A Santa Spirit Advent Calendar Book

COVID EDITION

Yvonne Vissing

Vissing & Associates

A SANTA SPIRIT
ADVENT
CALENDAR BOOK

Contents

Details	1
Introduction	2
Day 1 Build the Calendar	4
Day 2 Is Santa Real Scavenger Hunt	7
Day 3 Reindeer Hay	13
Day 4 Write to Santa	16
Day 5 Stars	20
Day 6 Santa Science	22
Day 8 Cookies!	25
Day 9 Puzzling Over Santa	33
Day 10 Holiday Card Creation	37
Day 11 Garland Magic	40
Day 12 Walky Talky	44
Day 13 Snowflakes Everywhere!	47

Day 14 Birds and Beasts	50
Day 15 Marshmallow People	59
Day 16 Santa Game Day	65
Day 17 Planning the Feastival	69
Day 18 If I Was Santa	73
Day 19 Trimming the Tree	76
Day 20 Book Trees	80
Day 21 Santa Movie Marathon	82
Day 22 Lifting Our Voices	84
Day 23 The Santa Stocking	88
Day 24 The Santa Feastival	100

Details

"CHRISTMAS, MY CHILD, IS LOVE IN ACTION. EVERY TIME WE LOVE, EVERY TIME WE GIVE, IT'S CHRISTMAS."
DALE EVANS
https://www.success.com/11-quotes-about-the-magic-of-christmas/

A Santa Spirit Advent Calendar Book ©
Yvonne Vissing 2020
Copyright Yvonne Vissing
All rights reserved.
No reproduction of book without author consent.
Copyright information 2020 Yvonne Vissing
Paperback ISBN 978-1-7358304-0-7
E-book ISBN 978-1-7358304-1-4
First edition 2020
Publisher Information: Vissing and Associates LLC
Vissing & Associates, LLC. PO Box 273 Chester NH.
Email vissingandassociates@gmail.com

$12.99

Introduction

A Santa Spirit Advent Calendar Book: COVID Edition is constructed to give families 24 days of activities that they can do at home, together as they prepare for the arrival of Santa! Activities are designed to bring joy and connection. They cost almost nothing except a little time and lots of love. This book is filled with hands-on, ready-to-do fun things that families can enjoy together. It is designed for busy parents who want to create happy holidays for their families without paying a lot of money or doing a lot of work. Inside you will find things that are:

Family-Friendly Fun
Promoting Togetherness
Happy Memory Building
Easy-to-do
Child-Engaged
Requiring Minimal/No Expense
Designed for Busy Families
Home-Based so you don't have to go anywhere

A traditional Advent calendar has 24 windows to open

leading up to Christmas. Many people do not celebrate Christmas for economic, religious or political reasons. Santa Claus is a secular figure found around the world that can be easily crafted to be diverse and inclusive, thus meeting the demands of contemporary society. This book seeks to transform Santa Claus from a person who brings material objects to the **spirit of loving-kindness** that anyone, and everyone, can create and share. The **Santa Spirit Advent Calendar Book: COVID Edition** contains readings from famous authors, quick-and-easy art projects, festive decorations that people of all ages can do and enjoy. Imagine each day the family sitting down together to do something fun to help them prepare their homes – and their hearts – for the spirited arrival of Santa. The bar for what constitutes a great Christmas seems to get higher and higher. Parents may cringe thinking of all it takes to create a happy holiday. COVID-19 has made it even harder for people who were just scraping by to get by.

But there is hope. This book helps parents to create merry holidays and happy memories for their children. It gives parents dozens of things you can do to prepare for the arrival of Santa that are enjoyable, inexpensive, and easy to do. Some are quick and some take a bit more time. You will find something to do each night. You don't have to do them in order. You can pick and choose what works best for your family, or take the ideas presented and tweak them to your heart's content! The essential ingredient in all of them is love, the essential component of the Santa Spirit. So go have fun! Be an elf! Happy memories await!

Day 1 Build the Calendar

Description: This activity is to introduce the Santa Spirit Advent Calendar. Frame the next 24 days to create a family expectation that you will be doing something special together each day to make a fun holiday. You will explain what the Santa Spirit is and show them how to use it to construct wonderful December festivities. The family can decide how to build and decorate the Santa Spirit Advent Calendar. Using household objects to build the calendar demonstrates that we can transform everyday things into something special. Once the calendar is constructed, you can put into each "day" a hint about what they will be doing. You can also tuck in pieces of candy, gum, notes or tiny objects if you so desire. Create the expectation that you will do something fun every day.

Materials & Execution: Consider things you have at home that you could use to build the calendar. Don't make the task too hard or too complex, and do not get caught wanting it to look a certain way. Don't be a perfectionist! Let it be organic. Remember that anticipating having FUN together every day is the goal.

Option 1: Paper Lunch Bag Calendar: Take 25 small paper bags and let everyone decorate them any way they please! Tape them on a door or wall in the shape of a pyramid or Christmas tree. Tuck into each bag instructions for the next Santa Spirit activity or whatever you like!

Option 2: Toilet Paper Tube Advent Calendar: Everyone has left-over toilet paper or paper towel tubes. Paper towel tubes can be cut into thirds. Fold one end over and tape it shut, giving it a bottom. This will enable you to put a note, treat or activity into the tube. Decorate the tubes with paint, glued-on paper pieces, glitter, fabric, markers, or whatever you choose. Then the tubes can be numbered and put into a basket or other area where they can be visibly seen and easily accessed each day.

Option 3: Can or Box Christmas Tree Advent Calendar: Everyone has things in the cupboard that can be saved to build the calendar, like plastic containers, empty boxes, or empty (clean) cans. They can be different sizes. Decorate them to look festive. You can paint the cans any way that pleases the individual artists! Decorate with paper (plain or construction), markers, crayons, pencils, paints, glitter, material, yarn, or whatever you have handy! You can adjust the "tree" by using bigger containers at the bottom to make the base. Then add progressively smaller containers on the next rows until there is only one at the top, making it in the shape of a pyramid or Christmas tree. Secretly, fill the "tree" containers with surprises of what the activity is going to be for that night. As the containers get opened and the "tree" gets smaller, it gives children a visual of how many more days they have to wait before Santa arrives!

Option 4: The Whatcha Got? Calendar: You can make a calendar out of anything! Use your imagination! And if all creativity fails, you can simply decorate envelopes.

Reading: What Is the Santa Spirit? By Yvonne Vissing

Santa Claus has existed for hundreds of years, bringing joy to families everywhere. Santa has gone by different names in different places. Santas could be male or female, old or young. Santa has sometimes looked tall or short, chubby or skinny with different skin tones. Usually Santas wear red and white hats, but not always. It's not what they look like that matters. The thing all Santas have in common is they share the Santa Spirit. The Santa Spirit is one of joy and loving-kindness. Santas work hard to find happiness inside and to make life better for other people. Santa Claus is not found in the presents they bring – the Santa Spirit is found in our helpful, happy hearts. Every day, let's see how many ways we can find the Santa Spirit! As we do our Santa Spirit Advent Calendar each day, let's talk about all the ways we have brought the Santa Spirit to others - and how it has been shared with us. Then when Santa comes in 24 days (or whenever you decide), it will be much more fun for us and everyone!

Day 2 Is Santa Real Scavenger Hunt

Description: Today create a scavenger hunt in your house or yard that engages children in the search for things related to Santa. Put notes and objects here and there in a scavenger hunt that leads them to a paper and markers where they can draw what they think Santa looks like. The focus of this activity is to have fun while we question where Santa can be found. Whether Santa is real has caused some parents difficulty because they want their children to believe he is real but they don't want to lie to them. This activity is designed to put that problem to rest. There is a way to enable children to believe in that Santa is real without lying to them. Children have the ability to believe in fantasy and reality at the same time; they know Mickey Mouse isn't a rodent and understand Big Bird can't fly. But they can still believe in them and enjoy them. Fantasy characters, including Santa, can teach children that things can be real in one way but not in another. If children don't ask you if he's real, give them time to figure it out themselves. If they do ask you, you must be honest but gentle, saying something like:

I believe that Santa's spirit exists and helps people to be nice to each other.

I got presents from Santa when I was little, so I always figured he was real.

I think that Santa is real, but he may not be real like you and me.

I believe in Santa (if you do, in some way).

Santa is considered a transitional figure who means different things to us at different points in our life. He is also a bridge between the concrete and abstract worlds. Santa as a human being could not live hundreds of years or travel the entire world with flying reindeer in a single night. But imagining how the possible could be possible is where scientific thought begins. Besides, it's fun to imagine that he could do wondrous things!

Materials & Execution: Scavenger hunts are so much fun and cost nothing. Simply, you write down a clue and have people figure out where it is and go to that location, where they find another clue that takes them somewhere else, and so on until they arrive at their destination – which for this activity could be drawing pictures of what Santa looks like to them and discussing whether he is real. The scavenger hunt can be so much fun that you could do one each day in to find the Santa Spirit in Advent Calendar activities or incorporate one each year ahead to create fun family Santa scavenger hunt traditions!

In the website Between Us Parents they have 70 different

Santa scavenger hunt clues you can adopt http://betweenus-parents.com/christmas-scavenger-hunt-clues/ but of course you can make up your own. Some of them include:

Santa Clue wears a bright suit made of red. Now go look where you rest your head.

Santa's white beard shows us he's pretty old. Your next clue can be found where we keep the food cold.

When you mail a letter to Santa, you have to use a stamp. Shine a light on this hunt and look by a _____.

To stay on Santa's nice list, you can't be a grouch. The next clue is under a cushion on the _____.

The anticipation builds as Santa draws nearer. Reflect on the next clue when you look in the _____.

On Dasher, Santa calls each reindeer by name. Your next clue can be found behind a picture _____.

Rudolph is the star with millions of fans. See what you find in the kitchen where we keep pots and _____.

Christmas isn't just about gifts, it's about moments we share. Find the next clue under the _____.

The children were nestled in their beds, nice and snug. Now look on the floor underneath the _____.

Dasher and Dancer are pros, not rookies. Go look where we keep Santa's _____.

This Good Housekeeping link provides plenty of inspirations for how to make a variety of scavenger hunts. https://www.goodhousekeeping.com/life/parenting/g32050844/scavenger-hunt-ideas-for-kids/

Here are other links with special Santa scavenger hunt

ideas: House Beautiful https://www.housebeautiful.com/lifestyle/a29003089/christmas-scavenger-hunt/ and Chicago Nhttp://www.chicagonow.com/between-us-parents/2014/12/printable-christmas-scavenger-hunt-clues/

At the last stop in this culmination of this activity, everyone in the family is to draw a picture of what Santa looks like or means to them. Undoubtedly, everyone will draw something different. This will help children to realize that Santa can look like lots of things and can generate interesting conversations about reality being variable.

Reading: Yes, Virginia, There Is a Santa Claus by Francis Church

In 1897 eight-year-old Virginia O'Hanlon wrote to the New York Sun newspaper. She had asked her father if there was a Santa, and her father suggested that she write to the newspaper, which was obliged only to state the truth. She wrote:

> **I am 8 years old. Some of my little friends say there is no Santa Claus. Papa says, "If you see it in The Sun, it's so." Please tell me the truth, is there a Santa Claus? Virginia O'Hanlon**

The newspaper's editor, Francis P. Church, wrote an editorial to the child in the paper – an editorial that has become famous. Here it is:

Virginia, your little friends are wrong. They have been affected by the skepticism of a skeptical age. They do not believe except what they see. They think that nothing can be which is not comprehensible by their little minds. All minds, Virginia, whether they be men's or children's, are little. In this great universe of ours, man is a mere insect, an ant, in his intellect as compared with the boundless world about him, as measured by the intelligence capable of grasping the whole of truth and knowledge.

Yes, Virginia, there is a Santa Claus.

He exists as certainly as love and generosity and devotion exist, and you know that they abound and give to your life its highest beauty and joy. Alas! how dreary would be the world if there were no Santa Claus! It would be as dreary as if there were no Virginias. There would be no childlike faith then, no poetry, no romance to make tolerable this existence. We should have no enjoyment, except in sense and sight. The external light with which childhood fills the world would be extinguished.

Not believe in Santa Claus! You might as well not believe in fairies. You might get your papa to hire men to watch in all the chimneys on Christmas eve to catch Santa Claus, but even if you did not see Santa Claus coming down, what would that prove? Nobody sees Santa Claus, but that is no sign that there is no Santa Claus. The most real things in the world are those that neither children nor men can see. Did you ever see fairies dancing on the lawn? Of course not, but that's no proof that they are not there. Nobody can conceive or imagine all the wonders there are unseen and unseeable in the world.

You tear apart the baby's rattle and see what makes the

noise inside, but there is a veil covering the unseen world which not the strongest man, nor even the united strength of all the strongest men that ever lived could tear apart. Only faith, poetry, love, romance, can push aside that curtain and view and picture the supernal beauty and glory beyond. Is it all real? Ah, Virginia, in all this world there is nothing else real and abiding.

No Santa Claus? Thank God he lives and lives forever. A thousand years from now, Virginia, nay 10 times 10,000 years from now, he will continue to make glad the heart of childhood. Merry Christmas and a Happy New Year!!!!

Day 3 Reindeer Hay

Description: There's nothing to perk up spirits than being creative (and a little messy) while making something sweet to eat together! Kitchens are great places for family and friends to congregate. Here is a no-bake cooking activity with loads of flexibility for everyone to make something different out of the same basic ingredients. Through combining your choice of chocolates or marshmallows with chow Mein noodles or pretzel sticks, you can mold them into shapes with a spoon or buttered hands to create an edible Santa display! You could create snow, mountains that Santa's sleigh can fly over, hay piles for reindeer or edible trees. Color some noodles red and mold them into Santa caps with white chocolate or marshmallow trim. Let your imagination loose!

Materials & Execution: Have available the following ingredients:

Chow Mein Noodles and/or Pretzel Sticks

Butterscotch bits, Chocolate chips, White chocolate, and/or mini marshmallows

Green food coloring if you want to make trees, red food coloring to make Santa hats

Colored sprinkles, silver candies or cinnamon dots

Peanuts, almond slivers or walnut pieces if you want

Wax paper or aluminum foil Butter for fingers to mold the displays

Steps: Roll out wax paper or aluminum foil for where you will create your figures. You need to create a gooey base for construction. In the microwave or double-boiler, melt your choice of white or dark chocolate bits, butterscotch bits, or marshmallows. Melt only one color of chocolate at a time – you can make multiple batches using different chocolates to create a variety of different delights! With a spoon, add in chow Mein noodles and/or pretzels while the gooey base is warm. Work swiftly to get the noodles covered. Pour it into a bowl or onto the wax paper where everyone can get to it. The concoction will be hot at first so let it get cool enough to handle if making figures, or use the spoon to daub some out to make butterscotch reindeer hay stacks. After you create the shapes or designs you want, you can add sprinkles to be ornaments on trees, faces for snow people, rocks for the mountains, or eyes for reindeer with red cinnamon noses and pretzel stick legs. You can put all your creations together and take a picture to send to relatives – if they last that long! They are truly delicious! And gluten-free! Here are some websites and YouTube to inspire your creations by Spruce Eats and Betty Crocker:

https://www.thespruceeats.com/haystacks-microwave-candy-chow-mein-noodles-3052388

https://www.bettycrocker.com/recipes/white-chocolate-haystacks/d3e902da-efba-4bc6-a669-bed1742f6152

Reading: Santa Claus is Coming to Town by John Coots and Haven Gillespie

> You better watch out You better not cry
> You better not pout I'm telling you why
> Santa Claus is coming to town
> He's making a list, Checking it twice,
> Gonna find out who's naughty or nice.
> Santa Claus is coming to town
> He sees you when you're sleeping
> He knows when you're awake
> He knows if you've been bad or good
> So be good for goodness sake
> With little tin horns, little toy drums
> Rooty toot toots and rummy tum tums
> Santa Claus is coming to town
> And curly head dolls that toddle and coo
> Elephants, boats, and kiddie cars too
> Santa Claus is comin' to town
> Then kids in Girls and Boy land will have a jubilee
> They're gonna build a Toyland town
> all around the Christmas tree
> So! You better watch out, you better not cry
> Better not pout, I'm telling you why
> Santa Claus is comin' to town

Day 4 Write to Santa

Description: Writing a letter to Santa is a useful family activity that has many benefits. First, it allows us to prioritize what we really need or want. Second, Santa appreciates receiving a well-written letter, and learning how to write a nice letter is something children can use forever. Third, as the family writes letters together, they can hear what each other desires. Since we are focusing on how to spread the Santa Spirit, role-model appropriate requests. Ask for few but meaningful things that aren't costly. If you put a bunch of expensive requests in your letter to Santa, you'd better be prepared to see your children follow suit in coming years!

Materials & Execution: Have paper to write on and something to write with – pens, pencils, crayons or markers. Also Envelopes that you buy or make. This activity will create more family bonding if you all write letters together at the same time. Here is a template parents can share about

HOW TO WRITE A GOOD LETTER TO SANTA

Greeting: Every letter should start with a pleasant greeting, such as "Dear Santa. I hope you are doing well. Are the reindeer ready for their trip?"

The Request: State what you would like Santa to bring and why. This should be reasoned and not greedy. Telling Santa why you have asked for a particular something is useful to Santa (and for the person writing the letter!).

Thank you for your consideration section: Santa is busy and isn't obligated to bring anything to anyone. Therefore, be polite and respectful. Thank Santa for consideration of your request. Express gratitude. Sign your name. Use good handwriting. This may mean re-writing the letter to look neat. Nobody wants to get a messy letter. Pictures are fine to draw as Santa likes art!

Reading: A Letter from Santa Claus by Mark Twain (real name Samuel Clemens)

My Dear Susie Clemens, I have received and read all the letters which you and your little sister have written me...I can read your and your baby sister's jagged and fantastic marks without any trouble at all....[last year] I went down your chimney at midnight when you were asleep and delivered [presents]...and kissed both of you, too...But...there were...one or two small orders which I could not fill because we ran out of stock...There was a word or two in your ... letter which...I took to be "a trunk full of doll's clothes." Is that it? I will call at your kitchen door about nine o'clock this morning to inquire. But I must not see anybody and I must not speak to anybody but you. ... you must go up to the nursery and stand on a chair or the bed and put your ear to the speaking tube that leads down to the kitchen and when I whistle through it you must speak in the tube and say, "Welcome, Santa Claus!" Then I will ask whether it was a trunk you ordered or not. If you say it was, I shall ask you what color you want the trunk to be...and then you must tell me every single thing in detail which you want the trunk to contain. Then when I say "Good-by and a merry Christmas to my little Susy Clemens," you must say "Good-by, good old Santa Claus, I thank you very much." ... I will go to the moon and get those things and.... I will come down the chimney that belongs to the fireplace that is in the hall...I couldn't get such a thing as a trunk down the nursery chimney, you know... If my boot should leave a stain on the marble, [do not clear] it away. Leave it there always in memory of my visit; and whenever you look at it or show it to anybody you must let it remind you to be a good little girl. Whenever you are naughty and someone points to that mark which your good old Santa Claus's boot made on the marble, what will you say, little sweetheart? Good-by for a few minutes, till I come down to the world and ring the kitchen doorbell.

Your loving Santa Claus Whom people sometimes call "The Man in the Moon"

Parent processing recommendation: Decide ahead of time how you are going to handle the letters. Some post offices have volunteers who answer children's letters - check with yours! Many communities or stores have a special "mailbox" available where letters to Santa can be dropped off. Some families put their letters in the chimney, on a window sill, or other location where one of Santa's helpers (like you) can pick them up. Some families choose to create a ritual where everyone puts their letters into the glowing fireplace, woodstove, bonfire, or candle so their messages can be sent aloft into the sky. Some parents opt to keep their children's letters to Santa in a secret place where they add to them year after year. Then when their children are grown, they wrap them up and return them as a special gift. Twain's letter to his daughter reminds her that he wished he could go to the moon and back to make his children happy – but it reminded her that sometimes he can't deliver everything children want. The letter ends reminding the child that she is always good and loved, even when she's a bit naughty.

Day 5 Stars

Description: Stars adorn the heavens. They have been present in almost every December holiday celebration around the world. Paper stars are easy and fun to make! All you need are lunch-size or smaller bags and glue!

Materials & Execution: For this activity, approximately 12 lunch bags are needed to make a star. Brown lunch bags can be purchased at most grocery stores for not much money. You can use colored or smaller paper bags. Glue sticks, paste or a glue gun is needed, scissors if you want to snip designs into the bags, crayons, markers, paints if you want to draw designs or put messages on the bags, glitter or other items to "fancy-up" your stars and string so you can hang them. To make the stars:

1. Count out 12 bags.
2. Color or draw on them if you want
3. Add glue to the flat face of the first bag.
4. Place a second bag on top facing the same direction and press down to make sure they stick together.
5. Repeat this process gluing together all the bags.

6. Optional: Snip small sections here and there in the bags
7. Fan them out to make the star
8. Add glue to the flat face of the top bag to the bottom bag
9. Add paint, glitter, or other decorations if you want
10. Tape on a string to hang them where you want

Here are YouTubes to show you how to make them:
https://www.youtube.com/watch?v=tPH2eVLEtco
https://www.youtube.com/watch?v=NjDj85b0dxA
https://www.youtube.com/watch?v=C8ETYDgax44

Reading: Star Light by Anonymous

Star light
Star bright
First star I see tonight
I wish I may
I wish I might
Have the wish
I wish tonight

Parent processing recommendation: Go outside and make wishes. Dreams inspire us and give us hope. Remind children that we can keep our wishes to ourselves. This gives children a sense of agency and that we all have a right to have our own dreams.

Day 6 Santa Science

Description: It's fun to figure out how Santa can do all the awesome things he does. Some adults get caught on "should I tell my children the truth about Santa?" But what IS the truth? Let children have fun figuring out for themselves how impossible things might be possible. In this activity, first ask the questions below and then engage everyone to explore big questions about Santa Claus. Create rules for the discussion before you begin. This will teach children about how to fairly manage a discussion with a group of people, which is a useful skill for anyone to learn and use in life!

Materials & Execution: This is a discussion night. Have paper and markers available so people can doodle during the discussion. And tasty snacks always make any conversation more delightful. Read the questions below to the people assembled. This will get them all thinking in the same direction before the discussion begins. The goal of this activity is not to prove what anyone says as "right" or "wrong", but to have fun playing with ideas about the many different ways some of the Santa events could occur! Be ready, able and willing to have fun being a discussion leader engaging family and friends in a light-hearted discussion about mysteries underlying Santa

Claus. If people lose perspective, remind them that this activity is just for fun! This will teach children the process of how to discuss and debate with others in a fair way. Consider writing down a list of Discussion Guidelines. Have everyone participate in the creation of the guidelines. Some may include: "We want to hear what everybody thinks. Don't let one person "hog" the conversation. No fighting or arguing. Disagree politely."

Here are some questions to start with, but let the crowd brainstorm other ideas:

Where is Santa from? While North Pole is a common answer, is it North Pole Alaska, Oklahoma, Idaho, or New York? There's also a North Pole in Australia, where Santa's sleigh is reportedly drawn by kangaroos, not reindeer! Some say he comes from Turkey, Iceland, Finland, Canada, Sweden, Greenland, or other places.

How does Santa get supplies in to his workshop to make the toys?

What are elves, what do they look like, where do they come from, what do they eat, what kinds of jobs do they have, etc. Can humans be elves or elf-helpers?

Can reindeer really fly? (According to Robert Sullivan's book, *Flight of the Reindeer*, some leap so high it seems like they fly…)

How does Santa know what you want? How does he decide what to give you? Is he a mind-reader? How does he read all those letters?

How can he get around the world in a single night? (Explore time zones, light speed, super-charged engine, etc.).

How can he fit everything for everyone into the sleigh?

If Santa comes down the chimney, **what does he do if someone doesn't have a fireplace**? How can he (or anyone) fit down a chimney? Is that safe?

Belief in Santa. Santa gives us an annual opportunity to consider just how the impossible might be possible. Scientists do that all the time. Come up with examples.

Your children will have other questions and ideas. Run with them! Explore them, even the silliest ones. The idea is to have fun.

Reading: Explore these quotes or the questions above:

Christmas is a necessity. There has to be at least one day of the year to remind us that we're here for something else besides ourselves.
Eric Severeid

It's Christmas Eve. It's the one night of the year when we all act a little nicer, we smile a little easier, we cheer a little more. For a couple of hours out of the whole year, we are the people that we always hoped we would be.
Frank Cross, "Scrooged"
https://www.goodhousekeeping.com/holidays/christmas-ideas/g1233/christmas-quotes/

Day 8 Cookies!

Description: Santa Claus isn't the only one who likes cookies – we ALL love cookies! In many homes people bake one of their favorites and then do a cookie swap. Others like to have friends and family over and do a marathon cookie-baking day. Many keep their favorites a family secret, something passed down from to new generations. Cookies are symbolic; we consumer memories of our cultures and our histories when we eat them. The beauty of baking cookies together is that we all get to be involved and learn the detailed "how-to's". Sharing conversations that occur while we are make the cookies. can be quite delicious! Laughing together, licking fingers, eating raw dough, smelling the wonderful aromas, and taking them off the pan and putting them onto a plate to decorate or eat is a process that is far better than munching on one that someone else made. The goal in this activity is to have fun together, make something tasty, and create positive memories. Pick the kind of cookies that warm your heart, as well as your belly!

Materials Needed & Execution: Choose a favorite family recipe that you want to pass on to your children. While chocolate chip cookies may be your go-to cookie, you may want to consider baking something that will be YOUR special holiday cookie that perhaps you make as a once-a-year delight. Remember, it doesn't matter what you make as much as what you make about it! Here are two family favorites you may want to try:

Buckeyes

Materials: Peanut butter, powdered sugar, butter, chocolate chips, wax paper. These are more candy than cookies. Cream soft butter together with creamy peanut butter. Use 2-3 times the amount of peanut butter compared to regular butter. When they are blended together, mix in the powdered sugar a bit at a time. Soon it will look like soft dough. Be careful not to add too much powdered sugar or the dough will get crumbly. Pull a bit of the dough out with clean hands and roll it into a ball. Children LOVE doing this! Put the balls onto a plate or cookie sheet covered with wax paper. Then pop them into the fridge until they are firm. While they are cooling, melt chocolate chips, either in a double boiler or in the microwave. When the chocolate is smooth, dip the peanut butter balls into it with a toothpick and return it to the wax paper. They look very pretty that way. If the balls are too soft, you may find it easier to keep them on the wax paper and then spoon the chocolate over the top of them. When the balls are covered with chocolate put them back into the fridge until firm. They are so delicious that they will disappear in a flash, so a word of advice is to make more than you think you'll need. You'll be glad you did!

Sugar Cookies

These are the classic Christmas cookie. There are many different recipes, but here is mine. Tweak it as desired! Ingredients include:

Flour (wheat or gluten free) White sugar Butter

Vanilla or almond extract Baking powder 1-2 eggs

Rolling pin and mat Cookie cutters or knife Sprinkles

Icing (home made with powdered sugar, butter and milk or ready-made)

Mix 1 stick of soft butter with 1 egg and 1 ½ cup of sugar. Add almond or vanilla extract. When that is mixed well, add 1 tsp of baking powder. Then add flour a bit at a time. You want it to be easy to handle but too much flour will make them hard. When it seems workable, put the dough on a floured mat and then roll it out with the rolling pin. Cut out shapes with a knife or cookie cutters. Then put the cookies on the cookie sheet and into a 350-degree oven. How long you bake them depends on how thick your dough is, but it's better to have them light and not too dark or they will be harder – unless you like cookies more crunch than cake-like. When they are cool, ice them and then decorate them to your hearts content! It is such fun for children to use a variety of sprinkles or icing that has food color in it to make tasty and beautiful designs.

Reading: A Christmas Inspiration by Lucy Maud Montgomery (of Anne of Green Gables)

"Well, I really think Santa Claus has been very good to us all," said Jean Lawrence, pulling the pins out of her heavy coil of fair hair and letting it ripple over her shoulders. "So do I," said Nellie Preston as well as she could with a mouthful of chocolates. "Those blessed home folks of mine seem to have divined by instinct the very things I most wanted." It was the dusk of Christmas Eve and they were all in Jean Lawrence's room at No. 16 Chestnut Terrace. No. 16 was a boarding-house, and boarding-houses are not proverbially cheerful places in which to spend Christmas, but Jean's room, at least, was a pleasant spot, and all the girls had brought their Christmas presents in to show each other. Christmas came on Sunday that year and the Saturday evening mail at Chestnut Terrace had been an exciting one. Jean had lighted the pink-globed lamp on her table and the mellow light fell over merry faces as the girls chatted about their gifts. On the table was a big white box heaped with roses that betokened a bit of Christmas extravagance on somebody's part. Jean's brother had sent them to her from Montreal, and all the girls were enjoying them in common. No. 16 Chestnut Terrace was overrun with girls generally. But just now only five were left; all the others had gone home for Christmas, but these five could not go and were bent on making the best of it. Belle and Olive Reynolds could not go home for Christmas because a young brother had measles….Beth …and Nellie…were art students, and their homes were too far away to visit… Jean was an orphan and had no home of her own…. "The postman… bulged with parcels. They were sticking out in every direction." "We all got our share of them," said Jean with a sigh of content. "Even the cook got six--I counted." "Miss

Allen didn't get a thing--not even a letter," said Beth quickly. Beth had a trick of seeing things that other girls didn't. "I forgot Miss Allen. No, I don't believe she did," answered Jean thoughtfully as she twisted up her pretty hair. "How dismal it must be to be so forlorn as that on Christmas Eve.... I'm glad I have friends." "I saw Miss Allen watching us as we opened our parcels and letters," Beth went on. "I happened to look up once, and such an expression as was on her face, girls! It was pathetic and sad and envious all at once. It really made me feel bad--for five minutes," she concluded honestly. "Hasn't Miss Allen any friends at all?" asked Beth. "No, I don't think she has," answered Jean. "She has lived here for 14 years...Nobody ever comes to see her and she never goes anywhere," said Beth. "Dear me! She must feel lonely now when everybody else is being remembered by their friends. I can't forget her face tonight; it actually haunts me. Girls, how would you feel if you hadn't anyone belonging to you, and if nobody thought about you at Christmas?" "Ow!" said Olive, as if the mere idea made her shiver. A little silence followed. To tell the truth, none of them liked Miss Allen. They knew that she did not like them either, she considered them frivolous and pert, and complained when they made a racket...Jean said with a dramatic flourish, "Girls, I have an inspiration--a Christmas inspiration!" "What is it?" cried four voices... "Let us give Miss Allen a Christmas surprise. She has not received a single present and I'm sure she feels lonely. Just think how we would feel if we were in her place." "That is true," said Olive thoughtfully. "Do you know, girls, this evening I went to her room with a message ...I do believe she had been crying. Her room looked dreadfully bare and cheerless, too. I think she is very poor. What are we to do, Jean?" "Let us each give her something nice. We can put the things just outside of her door so that she will see them whenever she opens it. I'll give her some of Fred's roses too, and I'll write a Christmassy letter in my very best style to go with them," said Jean, warming up to her ideas as she talked. The other girls caught her spirit and entered into the plan with enthusiasm. "Splendid!" cried Beth. "Jean, it is an inspiration, sure enough. Haven't we been horribly selfish--thinking of nothing but our own gifts and fun and pleasure? I really feel ashamed." "Let us do the thing up the very best way we can," said Nellie, forgetting even her beloved chocolates in her eagerness. "The shops are open yet. Let us go up town and invest." Five minutes later five capped and jacketed figures were scurrying up the street in the frosty, starlit December dusk. Miss Allen in her cold little room heard their gay voices and sighed. She was crying by herself in the dark. It was Christmas for everybody but her, she thought drearily. In an hour the girls came back with their purchases. "Now, let's hold a council...I hadn't the faintest idea what Miss Allen would like so I just guessed wildly. I got her a lace handkerchief and a big bottle of perfume and a painted photograph frame--and I'll stick my own photo in it for fun. That was really all I could afford. Christmas purchases have left my purse dreadfully lean." "I got her a glove-box and a pin tray," said Belle, "and Olive got her a calendar and [book of] poems. And...we are going to give her half of that big plummy fruit cake Mother sent us from home. I'm sure she hasn't tasted anything so delicious for years... Beth [said she was going to paint her a picture. Nellie got her a.... box of chocolate creams, a gorgeously striped candy cane, a bag of oranges... "We've got a lot of pretty things," said Jean in a tone of satisfaction. "Now we must do them up nicely. Will you wrap them in tissue paper, girls, and tie them with baby ribbon--here's a box of it--while I write that letter?" While the others chatted over their parcels Jean wrote her letter, and Jean could write delightful letters.... "You must all sign it now," said Jean, "and I'll put it in one of those big envelopes...Outside of Miss Allen's door the ...girls silently arranged their gifts on the floor. "That's done," whispered Jean in a tone of satisfaction as they tiptoed back.... It was in the early morning that Miss Allen opened her door. But early as it was, another door down the hall was half open too and five rosy faces were peering cautiously out. The girls had been up for an hour for fear they would miss the sight and were all in Nellie's room, which commanded a view of Miss Allen's door. That lady's face was a study. Amazement, incredulity, wonder, chased each other over it, succeeded by a glow of pleasure. On the floor before her was a snug little pyramid of parcels topped by Jean's letter.... Miss Allen looked down the hall but saw nothing, for Jean had slammed the door just in time. Half an hour later when they were going down to breakfast Miss Allen came along the hall with outstretched hands to meet them. She had been crying again, but I think her tears were happy ones; and she was smiling now. A cluster of Jean's roses was pinned on her breast. "Oh, girls, girls," she said, with a little tremble in her voice, "I can never thank you enough. It was so kind and sweet of you. You don't know how much good you have done me." Breakfast was an unusually cheerful affair at No. 16 that morning. There was no skeleton at the feast and everybody was beaming. Miss Allen laughed and talked like a girl herself. "Oh, how surprised I was!" she said...."How lovely the world is," said Jean. "This is really the very happiest Christmas morning I have ever known," declared Nellie. "I never felt so really Christmassy in my inmost soul before." "I suppose," said Beth thoughtfully, "that it is because we have discovered for ourselves the old truth that it is more blessed to give than to receive. I've always known it, in a way, but I never realized it before." "Blessing on Jean's Christmas inspiration," said Nellie. "But, girls, let us try to make it an all-the-year-round inspiration, I say. We can bring a little of our own sunshine into Miss Allen's life as long as we live with her." "Amen to that!" said Jean heartily. "Oh, listen, girls--the Christmas chimes!" And over all the beautiful city was wafted the grand old message of peace on earth and good will to all the world.

Parent processing recommendation: Reinforce the idea that the girls found joy through giving the Santa Spirit.

Day 9 Puzzling Over Santa

Description: Santa is a puzzle himself! Let's do puzzles together – jigsaw, crossword, word searches and scrambles, and more! Puzzles are good for the brain, and good for building conversations and problem-solving. The goal is to do things together. There are online Santa games, but if you print off paper versions, everyone can sit together and do them at the same time and talk about them. You can also make up your own word scrambles. Puzzle options are endless, and free! Here are suggestions on how you can make them yourself, along with some links to help guide you.

Materials & Execution: This activity can build upon the theme of Day 6 which questioned how Santa can do all the magical things he does! The notion that life is a puzzle could be woven into conversation as people work puzzles that could include:

Jigsaw puzzles are great for sitting around and talking while people look for pieces. Perhaps you have some at home, or relatives will let you work one of theirs. Second-hand stores often have puzzles for cheap. You just need a table or clear spot to work them.

Paper Puzzles - The most common types are word search, word scrambles and crossword puzzles. Older family members can actually make up their own for younger family members to use! This is a great task for teens and older children to engage them in the process of creating family events.

Here are a few websites that have more Santa puzzles and games that you can download:

Santa Word Search – Here are ready-made examples for word searches.

https://www.thesprucecrafts.com/free-christmas-word-search-puzzles-1356278

https://thewordsearch.com/puzzle/125/santa-claus/

Santa Crossword Puzzles - Here are ready-made examples for crossword puzzles.

https://www.pinterest.com/pin/66780006953005760/

https://www.puzzles-to-print.com/christmas-puzzles/christmas-vocabulary-image-crossword.shtml

https://chickenscratchny.com/christmas-crossword-puzzle/

Santa Scramble: All you have to do is mix up Santa-type words on a page and give them to others to work. Make them easier for young children. Example:

Aants sucal_____ (Santa Claus)
Oyts_____ (Toys)
Derirenre_____ (Reindeer)

Here are some ready-made ones you may want to consider:

https://www.bigactivities.com/word_scrambles/christmas/super_hard/christmas4.php

https://seasonal.theteacherscorner.net/christmas/christmas-wordscramble1-key.pdf

http://www.wordgames.com/en/santa-puzzle.html

You may also find Santa puzzle books at discount and other stores.

Reading: This is a brain teaser for the family to figure out together. It is courtesy of https://www.brainbashers.com/showpuzzles.asp?puzzle=ZKRG

Santa's Reindeer

First, name all 9 of the reindeer.

Santa has left plans for his elves to determine the order in which the reindeer will pull his sleigh. Some of the reindeer have opinions about who they want to be next to. This year his elves are working to the following schedule, which will form a single line of nine reindeer. Can you help the elves work out the order of the reindeer?

Comet behind Rudolph, Prancer and Cupid.

Blitzen behind Cupid and in front of Donder, Vixen and Dancer.

Cupid in front of Comet, Blitzen and Vixen.

Donder behind Vixen, Dasher and Prancer.

Rudolph behind Prancer and in front of Donder, Dancer and Dasher.

Vixen in front of Dancer and Comet.

Dancer behind Donder, Rudolph and Blitzen.

Prancer in front of Cupid, Donder and Blitzen.

Dasher behind Prancer and in front of Vixen, Dancer and Blitzen.

Donder behind Comet and Cupid. Cupid in front of Rudolph and Dancer.

Vixen behind Rudolph, Prancer and Dasher.

The answer:

Prancer

Cupid

Rudolph

Dasher

Blitzen

Vixen

Comet

Donder

Dancer

Day 10 Holiday Card Creation

Description: Getting cards is fun! It reminds us that someone is thinking of us and wishing us a happy holiday. Messages contained in the cards can be sweet and loving, or funny and make us laugh. They can contain hope and sometimes presents, like pictures, poems, stories, money, gift cards, or trinkets. In olden days, people would decorate their homes with the cards they received. It made them happy every time they looked at them. This activity is designed to have the family sit together and decide to whom they want to send cards. Cards can be constructed either on paper or electronically. Figuring out what the cards should look like and what message each should send will help the family to talk about who matters to them and how to send them cheerful messages.

Materials & Execution: Ideally, the family could put aside a time when they all do their card-making together. It could be that each person may want to send greetings to some of the same people. This could allow for some coordination and conversation about what that person means to them. First make a list of people to get cards. Then find their address (phone for text card, email address for computerized card, or physical mailing address for US postal mail). Compile the list and save it in a safe manner so it can be accessed next year. Create the cards and decide when to mail them!

For **paper cards** have paper of various kinds, paints, markers, pencils, glitter, ribbons, etc. You can include photos or make pictures. Envelopes can be purchased or hand-made.

Here is Aloha Craft's website YouTube to inspire your card making:

https://www.youtube.com/watch?v=zC4gjIXhuLk

Country Living's: https://www.countryliving.com/diy-crafts/how-to/g3872/christmas-card-ideas/

and Better Homes & Gardens: https://www.bhg.com/christmas/cards/make-your-own-christmas-cards/

Online cards are easy if you have access to a computer, tablet or smart-phone. Computers give us the ability to design our own cards and messages, either through WORD, graphics programs, or access to free card programs like 123 Greeting cards https://www.123greetings.com/ Some online card programs offer unlimited free cards for a limited time, so having your list ready would be helpful! You can add pictures to your cards from your camera. Options are endless for making pretty, cool, fun, sentimental, or interesting cards.

Reading: Origins of the Holiday Greeting Card

The first Christmas card was reported to be a letter sent in Wales in 1611. Back then it was custom to write letters to people you cared about to wish them good cheer during the December holidays. But writing letters took a long time for people to pen, especially when they had lots of people they wanted to send holiday greetings to. In 1843 Sir Henry Cole in England commissioned John Calcott Horsley to paint a card that wished people a Merry Christmas and a Happy New Year. Soon it became custom to make and send holiday cards. People made their cards and each was unique. They may be decorated with satin, ribbons, lace or folded into fans and unusual shapes. Some were made into puzzles, others had pop-up images. Cards became so popular that Louis Prang opened a lithographic shop in 1875 and by 1881 sold over 5 million cards, thus establishing the custom of sending cards to people during special occasions and holidays like Christmas. And the rest is history!

http://www.emotionscards.com/museum/xmas.html

Day 11 Garland Magic

Description: Decorating homes in December has occurred over hundreds of years around the world for celebrations. Decorating helps signify the specialness of the time and welcoming to others. Beautifying them home helps children to learn how to make holidays special. Children are the gatekeepers to tomorrow. This activity is designed to involve everyone in the family to make easy, inexpensive decorations that can adorn trees, walls, doorways, or other areas. One of the easiest, cheapest and prettiest decorations to make are merry garlands.

Materials & Execution: Here are two different garlands that families can make. Choose one or choose all! Here are the materials for each of the choices:

Paper Garlands

Materials needed: Construction paper Scissors Tape or stapler. The simplest type is to cut **construction paper** into strips that are the same width and length. Often they are 1-1/2 inch -long strips. Coil the first strip and close with a staple or tape. Coil the second strip around the first and close with a staple or tape and keep going until the garland is the length you want. You can alternate colors if you want.

Descriptions of paper garlands can be found at websites like:

https://www.wikihow.com/Make-a-Paper-Garland

https://www.thesprucecrafts.com/paper-garlands-diy-4128813

https://yeswemadethis.com/10-creative-diy-paper-garland-ideas/

Cranberry and/or Popcorn Garlands

These are classic garlands that you can hang inside or put outside on the trees for the birds. Pop popcorn or purchase bags of ready-made popcorn (no salt type if putting out for the birds, please). String popped kernels together by using a large needle attached to thread or dental floss (for more strength). Tie at the end and put up as decoration. You can do the same thing with cranberries purchased in bags from the grocery. Or you can use a variation of the popcorn and cranberry garlands above by string together one (or more) of pieces of popcorn, followed by one (or more) cranberries. Repeat the pattern for as long as you wish. Tie off and put on the tree or wherever you wish.

Reading: How I'll Decorate *My* Tree By Liz Lochhead

It was still very far from Christmas When my momma said to me

Tell me, Precious, what you going to hang On our Christmas tree?

I said the fairy-lights that Dad just fixed! And... jewel-coloured jelly-beans from the

pick'n'mix. Oh, and from it I'll dangle tinsel in tangles, Sparkles, sequins and spangles,

A round golden coin (chocolate money), That cracker joke that was *actually funny.*

My rosary beads and a plastic rose as red as Rudolph Reindeer's nose,

The gnome that grows the tangerines, The picture of me with my tambourine,

And (Mum's favourite, she says) The photo of all of us in our PJ's

The Ladybird Book that Lola lent me,

The blue butterfly bracelet that Brittany sent me,

The ear-ring I lost, A pop-up Jack Frost,

A space-hopper, an everlasting gobstopper,

A pink-eyed sugar mouse, The keys to my Grandfather's house,

A tiny pair of trainers with silver laces, And now my smile is straight,

gonna hang up my braces! A marble, an angel-scrap, a star,

The very last sweetie out my Advent Calendar, A kiss under the mistletoe,

A mitten still cracked with a crunch and a creak of snow,

That glitter scarf I finally got sick of, A spoon with cake-mix still to lick off,

The Dove of Peace that our Darren made,

Some green thoughts in our tree's green shade I'll hang every evergreen memory

Of moments as melted and gone As that candle that was *supposed* to smell Of cinnamon

Memories big as a house and as small 's The baubles I used to call *ball-balls*

With pleasure I'll treasure them Then, on *proper* Christmas Day

I'll show them all to you Between the Queen's Speech and Doctor Who!

Parent processing recommendation: Have members talk about their favorite things about decorating the tree!

Day 12 Walky Talky

Description: Every day is different so going out into the world together gives us fresh air and new views to share. Walking encourages conversations which have a way of traveling to unexpected destinations. Depending on people's ability, the walk could be in the neighborhood and close to home, or the walk could be miles long. People in the city may enjoy walking past store-fronts to gaze at window displays. People in the mountains may go for a hike; those near the beach could have a picnic, or construct a sports or fitness opportunity that everyone does together. Time is a curious thing – we may spend too much time together or not enough. This activity focuses not so much on WHAT we do but HOW we do it! This is where the Santa Spirit comes into play! Invest in creating good conversations and positive memories with each other – there is no need to invest money in going out together and enjoying one another's company. If COVID subsides and we can go out in public, maybe we could go to indoor places. But until the virus is under control, physical distance from others, wear a mask, and do the honor of keeping yourself and others from getting exposed to risks. That is part of the Santa Spirit too.

Materials & Execution: Going outside together requires no purchases. Depending on how your family functions, you can create a surprise adventure for the family. It's fun to do something ordinary that is made special. It could result from a family conference when everyone talks about things they'd like to do and certain events get selected. Or it could be a spur of the moment situation where the time seems right to go do something together. Do whatever it takes to maximize the Santa Spirit's chances to grow in your hearts and homes. Be flexible to alter the plan when the need or opportunity arises. Make sure to create an event that people of all ages and abilities can enjoy.

Reading: A Precious Christmas Memory by Pat A. Fleming

In the damp, dusty cellar, surrounded by boxes, our excitement just grows without measure. Searching and sorting with loud shouts of glee we uncovered the grand Christmas treasure. Christmas lights in a ball, but Dad's not deterred. As with a purpose, he heads out the door. And I spy from the window, for the time has now come for Dad to adorn our front porch. The weather is frigid, his breath floats in the air and the sky is the deepest of gray. The spirit of Christmas can be felt everywhere with the promise of snow on the way. So I watch as my Dad makes his plan of attack while I sit comfy, cozy inside. But I knew in my heart where I needed to be, out there shivering, but right by his side. So I bundle up tight and I head out the door. Nothing can stand in my way. And I knew by his smile and his pat on my back that he truly was glad that I came. Now perfectionist Dad always knew what to do. For him every light had its place. So together we stood, completing our task, Precious memories these moments would make. Under an ominous sky large snowflakes appeared and it seemed that the time had just flown. But we both were determined to finish the job, though tired and chilled to the bone. As the last light was placed, complete darkness prevailed, we had accomplished our goal just in time. The smell of Mom's cooking floated by in the air and the feeling of success was sublime. Now into the house, I run with such joy to summon all family to come. And we stand on the street, as Dad plugs in the lights, Illuminating our world one by one. For certain it's Christmas and my heart feels so full with the beauty of color and shimmer. But being with Dad sharing time in the cold Is forever what I will remember!

Parent processing recommendation: Explore with everyone what kinds of family adventures they would like to continue to do. Then try to do as many as possible to build participation and family bonding.

Day 13 Snowflakes Everywhere!

Description: One of the easiest, and prettiest, winter decoration to make are snowflakes. Scientists have discovered looking at real snowflakes that fall from the sky that no two are alike. Everyone is different. So it is with paper snowflakes. Or people! The youngest of us who is just learning how to cut paper will have different looking snowflakes than the ornate ones that teenagers might create. The cool thing about snowflakes is they can go anywhere, hang from the ceiling, taped to windows, or everywhere one can imagine! And unlike icy snowflakes, these may be easier to clean up!

Materials & Execution: All you need is paper, scissors, and string or tape to hang the snowflakes up. You can add glitter or add color to them with markers. For nostalgia, play find the old song, "Here comes Suzy Snowflake" while you cut! https://www.youtube.com/watch?v=FEe6KOWdbUs or https://www.youtube.com/watch?v=PbJuqBkXrdM

The Traditional Snowflake: To make the simplest snowflake, take a piece of paper, fold it into a square 3 times, curve the big end and cut the tip off the little corner where the folds intersect. Or you can start by putting a plate down on the paper and drawing a circle, and then cutting out the circle and then folding it into a triangle. Cut the tip off. Then take the scissors and cut out little slivers into the folded paper. The cuts can be long or short, thin or wider (but not too wide!). Unfold and voila – a snowflake!

Websites that show you how include:

First Palette https://www.firstpalette.com/craft/paper-snowflake-4sides.html

Real Simple: https://www.realsimple.com/work-life/entertainment/crafts-hobbies/how-to-make-paper-snowflakes

Martha Stewart gives her version of how to make beautiful snowflakes, with diagrams, here! https://www.marthastewart.com/266694/decorating-with-paper-snowflakes

Snowflake Youtubes:

https://www.youtube.com/watch?v=59dOIF3PMjY

https://www.youtube.com/watch?v=YeR5p8OocUE

The 3-D Snowflake: These are a step-above the traditional snowflake and aren't really that hard to make! Check out these instructions on how to make them:

Wiki How https://www.wikihow.com/Make-a-3D-Paper-Snowflake

Instructables: https://www.instructables.com/id/3D-Paper-Snowflake-In-Four-Easy-Steps/

Here are some Youtubes on how to make them:

https://www.youtube.com/watch?v=lT2oeNkTOAk

https://www.youtube.com/watch?v=DOnc3gi9Rkc

Multi-Creative Snowflakes:

If you want to get really fancy, check out how to make Multi-Creative Snowflakes:

https://www.pinterest.com/justjennadesign/paper-snowflakes/

https://handsonaswegrow.com/make-snowflake-crafts/

https://happyhooligans.ca/25-snowflake-crafts-activities-treats/

https://www.notimeforflashcards.com/2017/01/snowflake-crafts-3-year-olds.html

Reading: Snowflakes by mrcshareseaseblog.wordpress

> Snowflakes, snowflakes
> Falling everywhere
> They stick to my nose
> They stick to my hair
> When one falls upon my hand
> And I look carefully
> I see that each one is unique
> Just like you and me.

Parent processing recommendation: Discuss unique attributes of snowflakes, people, or diversity in life as a natural follow-up. Helping each other to see the different types of beauty is important in finding the Santa Spirit.

Day 14 Birds and Beasts

Description: Many families include four-legged, finned and feathered friends. This activity is to help us remember to be generous and kind to our animal family. Santa relies upon his reindeer. Many animals and birds associated with Santa's arrival, including kangaroos who pull Santa's sleigh in Australia. The goal of this activity is to help make children aware of our interconnection with animals, birds, and other critters.

Materials & Execution: There are several different approaches that you can take for this activity. One is to celebrate your pets; millions of us have cats, dogs, horses, ferrets, reptiles, birds, fish, or other critters who are a part of our family. They count on us to feed and care for them. But outside our window is a world of animals who watch us every day that we may wish to pay more attention to. The sparrows, robins and cardinals who flock outside may appreciate if you put up a seed or suet feeder. The geese may like if you toss corn out for them to eat on their journey to warmer weather. There are deer, turkeys, ground hogs, bats, skunks, feral cats, and other animals whose habitats are being encroached that you could learn more about and help. Another way to approach this activity is to focus on the greater community of critters. Maybe you want to engage your family to do something for your local animal rescue society. Perhaps you want to volunteer to do something for a zoo, barn, stable, animal reserve, or other organization near your community. Maybe you want to offer to walk the dog of a neighbor who can't go out. There are national and international organizations that seek to help creatures that fly in the sky, roam the earth, or swim in the seas. Deciding how to help them would enable you to make merry by helping our 4-legged, finned and winged friends. Talk with your family. Decide which animals you want to help and how you want to do it. Then follow through on that plan, whether it is one-time, monthly, or an ongoing commitment to help the critters who depend on us.

Reading: Tilly's Christmas by Louisa May Alcott, author of *Little Women*

" I'm so glad to-morrow is Christmas, because I'm going to have lots of presents."
" So am I glad, though I don't expect any presents but a pair of mittens."
" And so am I; but I shan't have any presents at all."
As the 3 little girls trudged home from school they said these things, and as Tilly spoke, both the others looked at her with pity and some surprise, for she spoke cheerfully, and they wondered how she could be happy when she was so poor she could have no presents on Christmas.

" Don't you wish you could find a purse full of money right here in the path?" said Kate, the child who was going to have " lots of presents." ...

" What would you buy?" asked Bessy, rubbing her cold hands, longing for her mittens.

" I'd buy a pair of large, warm blankets, a load of wood, a shawl for mother, and a pair of shoes for me; and if there was enough left, I'd give Bessy a new hat, and then she needn't wear Ben's old felt one," answered Tilly. The girls laughed at that; but Bessy pulled the funny hat over her ears, and said she was much obliged, but she'd rather have candy.

" Let's look, and maybe we can find a purse. People are always going about with money at Christmas time, and someone may lose it here," said Kate. So, as they went along the snowy road, they looked about them, half in earnest, half in fun. Suddenly Tilly sprang forward, exclaiming, " I see it! I've found it! "

The others followed, but all stopped disappointed; for it wasn't a purse, it was only a little bird. It lay upon the snow with its wings spread and feebly fluttering, too weak to fly. Its little feet were benumbed with cold; its once bright eyes were dull with pain, and instead of a blithe song, it could only utter a faint chirp, now and then, as if crying for help.

" Nothing but a stupid old robin..." cried Kate..."I shan't touch it. I found one once, and took care of it, and the ungrateful thing flew away the minute it was well," said Bessy, creeping under Kate's shawl, and putting her hands under her chin to warm them.

" Poor little birdie! How pitiful he looks, and how glad he must be to see someone coming to help him! I'll take him up gently, and carry him home to mother. Don't be frightened, dear, I'm your friend;" and Tilly knelt down in the snow, stretching her hand to the bird with the tenderest pity in her face.

Kate and Bessy laughed ."Don't stop for that thing; it's getting late and cold: let's go on and look for the purse," they said, moving away.

" You wouldn't leave it to die?' cried Tilly. "I'd rather have the bird than the money, so I shan't look any more. The purse wouldn't be mine, and I should only be tempted to keep it; but this poor thing will thank and love me, and I'm so glad I came in time." Gently lifting the bird, Tilly felt its tiny cold claws cling to her hand, and saw its dim eyes brighten as it nestled down with a grateful chirp. "Now I've got a Christmas present after all," she said, smiling, as -they walked on. " I always wanted a bird, and this one will be such a pretty pet for me!"

" He'll fly away the first chance he gets, and die anyhow; so you'd better not waste your time over him," said Bessy.

" He can't pay you for taking care of him, and my mother says it isn't worthwhile to help folks that can't help us," added Kate.

" My mother says, do as you'd be done by; and I'm sure I'd like any one to help me if I was dying of cold and hunger. Love your neighbor as yourself is another of her sayings. This bird is my little neighbor, and I'll love him and care for him, as I often wish our rich neighbor would love and care for us," answered Tilly, breathing her warm breath over the benumbed bird, who looked up at her with confiding eyes...and know a friend.

" What a funny girl you are," said Kate; " caring for that silly bird, and talking about loving your neighbor in that sober way. Mr. King don't care a bit for you, and never will, though he knows how poor you are; so I don't think your plan amounts to much."

" I believe it, though; and shall do my part, anyway. Good-night. I hope you'll have a merry Christmas, and lots of pretty things," answered Tilly, as they parted. Her eyes were full, and she felt so poor as she went on alone toward the little old house where she lived. It would have been so pleasant to know that she was going to have some of the pretty things all children love to find in their full stockings on Christmas morning. And pleasanter still to have been able to give her mother something nice. So many comforts were needed, and there was no hope of getting them; for they could barely get food and fire.

" Never mind, birdie, we'll make the best of what we have, and be merry in spite of everything. You shall have a happy Christmas, anyway; and I know God won't forget us, if everyone else does." She stopped a minute to wipe her eyes, and lean her cheek against the bird's soft breast, finding great comfort in the little creature, though it could only love her, nothing more. " See, mother, what a nice present I've found," she cried, going in with a cheery face that was like sunshine in the dark room.

" I'm glad of that, dearie; for I haven't been able to get my little girl anything but a rosy apple. Poor bird! Give it some of your warm bread and milk."

" Why, mother, what a big bowlful! I'm afraid you gave

me all the milk," said Tilly, smiling over the nice, steaming supper that stood ready for her.

"I've had plenty, dear. Sit down and dry your wet feet, and put the bird in my basket on this warm flannel."

Tilly peeped into the closet and saw nothing there but dry bread. "Mother's given me all the milk, and is going without her tea, 'cause she knows I'm hungry. Now I'll surprise her, and she shall have a good supper too. She is going to split wood, and I'll fix it while she's gone." So Tilly put down the old tea-pot, carefully poured out a part of the milk, and from her pocket produced a great, plummy bun, that one of the school-children had given her, and she had saved for her mother. A slice of the dry bread was nicely toasted, and the bit of butter set by for her put on it. When her mother came in there was the table drawn up in a warm place, a hot cup of tea ready, and Tilly and birdie waiting for her.

Such a poor little supper, and yet such a happy one; for love, charity, and contentment were guests there, and that Christmas eve was a blither one than that up at the great house, where lights shone, fires blazed, a great tree glittered, and music sounded, as the children danced and played.

"We must go to bed early, for we've only wood enough to last over to-morrow. I shall be paid for my work the day after, and then we can get some," said Tilly's mother, as they sat by the fire.

"If my bird was only a fairy bird, and would give us three wishes, how nice it would be! Poor dear, he can't give me anything; but it's no matter," answered Tilly, looking at the robin, who lay in the basket with his head under his wing, a mere little feathery bunch.

"He can give you one thing, Tilly, the pleasure of doing good. That is one of the sweetest things in life; and the poor can enjoy it as well as the rich." As her mother spoke, with her tired hand softly stroking her little daughter's hair, Tilly suddenly started and pointed to the window, saying, in a frightened whisper,

" I saw a face, a man's face, looking in! It's gone now; but I truly saw it."

" Some traveler attracted by the light perhaps. I'll go and see." And Tilly's mother went to the door. No one was there. The wind blew cold, the stars shone, the snow lay white on field and wood, and the Christmas moon was glittering in the sky.

"What sort of a face was it?" asked Tilly's mother, coming back.

" A pleasant sort of face, I think; but I was so startled I don't quite know what it was like. I wish we had a curtain there," said Tilly.

" I like to have our light shine out in the evening, for the road is dark and lonely just here, and the twinkle of our lamp is pleasant to people's eyes as they go by. We can do so little for our neighbors, I am glad to cheer the way for them. Now put these poor old shoes to dry, and go to bed, dearie; I'll come soon."

Tilly went, taking her bird with her to sleep in his basket nearby, lest he should be lonely in the night. Soon the little house was dark and still, and no one saw the Christmas spirits at their work that night. When Tilly opened the door next morning, she gave a loud cry, clapped her hands, and then stood still, quite speechless with wonder and delight. There, before the door, lay a great pile of wood, all ready to burn, a big bundle and a basket; with a lovely nosegay of winter roses, holly, and evergreen tied to the handle.

"Oh, mother! did the fairies do it?" cried Tilly, pale with her happiness, as she seized the basket, while her mother took in the bundle.

"Yes, dear, the best and dearest fairy in the world, called 'Charity.' She walks abroad at Christmas time, does beautiful deeds like this, and does not stay to be thanked," answered her mother with full eyes, as she undid the parcel.

There they were, the warm, thick blankets, the comfortable shawl, the new shoes, and, best of all, a pretty winter hat for Bessy. The basket was full of good things to eat, and on the flowers lay a paper saying, "For the little girl who loves her neighbor as herself."

"Mother, I really think my bird is a fairy bird, and all these splendid things come from him," said Tilly, laughing and crying with joy. It really did seem so, for as she spoke, the robin flew to the table, hopped to the nosegay, and perching among the roses, began to chirp with all his little might. The sun streamed in on flowers, bird, and happy child, and no one saw a shadow glide away from the window; no one ever knew that Mr. King had seen and heard the little girls the night before, or dreamed that the rich neighbor had learned a lesson from the poor neighbor.

And Tilly's bird was a fairy bird; for by her love and tenderness to the helpless thing, she brought good gifts to herself, happiness to the unknown giver of them, and a faithful little friend who did not fly away, but stayed with her till the snow was gone, making summer for her in the winter-time.

Source: *Aunt Jo's Scrap-Bag*, Volume 1, *My Boys, And Other Stories*.
http://www.hymnsandcarolsofchristmas.com/Text/tillys_christmas.htm

Parent processing recommendation: Use this activity to inspire dedication to caring for the animals and the earth. Generate ideas for acts of loving kindness to them.

Day 15 Marshmallow People

Description: Marshmallow snow people are quick, easy, inexpensive and fun to make. They are also delicious! Young children can make simple ones; older people can construct more sophisticated people and snow people scenes. This activity only requires few ingredients and a spirit designed to make happy memories of this holiday season.

Materials & Execution: Put onto the table or cabinet bags of marshmallows. They come in different sizes, so having small, medium and large ones provides builders more options. Have all the decoration options and construction tools on the table as well.

Helpful ingredients to have on hand:

- Wooden skinny sticks or toothpicks – to hold the marshmallows together to be made into bodies, animals, or whatever you wish! Toothpicks are also useful to use as paintbrushes to dip into Food Col-

oring for eyes, mouths, and other decorations. Food color pens are an option.
- Sprinkles, cinnamon dots, M & M's, chocolate bits, and small candies are easy decorations to use as eyes, buttons, or anything imaginable! Candy like gummy candy can be flattened and made into scarfs, orange or red ones can be shaped into noses or smiles.
- Cookies or candy canes can be put together as sleds for the snow people to sit on*
- Pretzel sticks are good for antlers or arms!
- Oreo type cookies or upside down mini Reeses peanut butter cups can become hats, coconut for hair and other things, graham crackers for sleds, etc.
- Frosting makes for good glue to hold them together after it hardens a bit.

The Food Network shows how to make real marshmallows from scratch! Very delicious and good to show children that we don't have to go to the store to buy them! https://www.youtube.com/watch?v=TSx_ZqXlkI8

Here are some websites and Youtubes to inspire your creations:

Marshmallow snow people, edible variety: https://www.martysmusings.net/marshmallow-snowman-craft-can-eat/

Marshmallow reindeer:

https://www.justataste.com/chocolate-reindeer-marshmallow-pops-recipe/

https://www.suburbansimplicity.com/chocolate-covered-marshmallow-reindeer/

Marshmallow penguins:
https://www.pinterest.com/pin/547187423470593474/

Pinterest has lots of pictures of marshmallow creation sure to inspire your creative genius! https://www.pinterest.com/abosulit/marshmallow-snowman/

Here are a couple of You tubes of how to make marshmallow people:

https://www.pinterest.com/abosulit/marshmallow-snowman/

https://www.youtube.com/watch?v=BHO28m-QKic

Reading: Excerpts from **A Child's Christmas in Wales** by Dylan Thomas

One Christmas was so much like another, in those years around the sea-town corner…out of all sound except the distant speaking of the voices I sometimes hear a moment before sleep, that I can never remember whether it snowed for six days and six nights when I was twelve or whether it snowed for twelve days and twelve nights when I was six….

Years and years ago, when I was a boy, when there were wolves in Wales, and birds the color of red-flannel petticoats whisked past the harp-shaped hills, when we sang and wallowed all night and day in caves that smelt like Sunday afternoons in damp front farmhouse parlors, and we chased…the bears, before the motor car, before the wheel, before the duchess-faced horse, when we rode the daft and happy hills bareback, it snowed and it snowed. But here a small boy says: "It snowed last year, too. I made a snowman and my brother knocked it down and I knocked my brother down and then we had tea." "But that was not the same snow," I say. "Our snow was not only shaken from white wash buckets down the sky, it came shawling out of the ground and swam and drifted out of the arms and hands and bodies of the trees; snow grew overnight on the roofs of the houses like a pure and grandfather moss, minutely ivied the walls and settled on the postman, opening the gate, like a dumb, numb thunderstorm of white, torn Christmas cards."...

"And then the Presents...There were the Useful Presents: engulfing mufflers of the old coach days, and mittens made for giant sloths; zebra scarfs of a substance like silky gum that could be tug-o'-warred down to the galoshes; blinding tam-o'-shanters like patchwork tea cozies ... from aunts who always wore wool next to the skin...that made you wonder why the aunts had any skin left at all... And picture less books..."

"Go on the Useless Presents."

"Bags of moist and many-colored jelly babies and a folded flag and a false nose and a tram-conductor's cap and a machine that punched tickets and rang a bell... and a celluloid duck that made, when you pressed it, a most unducklike sound, a mewing moo that an ambitious cat might make who wished to be a cow; and a painting book in which I could make the grass, the trees, the sea and the animals any colour I pleased, and still the dazzling sky-blue sheep are grazing in the red field under the rainbow-billed and pea-green birds. Hardboileds, toffee, fudge and allsorts, crunches, cracknels, humbugs, glaciers, marzipan, and butterwelsh for the Welsh...And...Games for Little Engineers, complete with instructions. And a whistle to make the dogs bark to wake up the old man next door to make him beat on the wall with his stick to shake our picture off the wall....

"There are always Uncles at Christmas. The same Uncles.... Mistletoe hung from the gas brackets in all the front parlors; there was sherry and walnuts and...crackers by the dessertspoons; and cats in their fur-abouts watched the fires; and the high-heaped fire spat, all ready for the chestnuts... For dinner we had turkey and blazing pudding, and after dinner the Uncles sat in front of the fire, loosened all buttons, put their large moist hands over their watch chains, groaned a little and slept. Mothers, aunts and sisters scuttled to and fro, bearing tureens. Auntie Bessie, who had already been frightened, twice, by a clock-work mouse, whimpered at the sideboard and had some elderberry wine. I would blow up balloons to see how big they would blow up to; and, when they burst, which they all did, the Uncles jumped and rumbled. In the rich and heavy afternoon, the Uncles breathing like dolphins and the snow descending, I would sit among festoons and Chinese lanterns and nibble dates and try to make a model... following the Instructions for Little Engineers..Or I would go out, my bright new boots squeaking, into the white world, on to the seaward hill, to call on Jim and Dan and Jack and to pad through the still streets, leaving huge footprints on the hidden pavements....

Always on Christmas night there was music. An uncle played the fiddle, a cousin sang "Cherry Ripe," and another uncle sang "Drake's Drum." It was very warm in the little house.... and then I went to bed. Looking through my bedroom window, out into the moonlight and the unending smoke-colored snow, I could see the lights in the windows of all the other houses on our hill and hear the music rising from them up the long, steady falling night. I turned the gas down, I got into bed. I said some words to the close and holy darkness, and then I slept.

Parent Processing Recommendation: The famous Welsh poet Dylan Thomas wrote and recorded its original telling for the radio in 1952, in what became one of his most popular stories. ***A Child's Christmas in Wales*** is told by a young child romanticizing the simpler days of Christmases past. What are memories that you all share about what happens at holidays? This story sets up good family story-telling opportunities.

Day 16 Santa Game Day

Description: Part of the spreading the Santa Spirit requires that we play and games are a good way to do this. Playing games is good for our brains and forces us to put work aside while we enjoy one another. We can find joy teaching children how to play a game. Remember – don't take yourself or winning too seriously! This is where the Santa Spirit of generosity and joy become paramount. Types of games we can play are endless; it doesn't matter what type so long as everyone is having fun together.

Materials & Execution: What's your favorite games you love to play? On Santa Game Day it is advisable to let everyone pick one game that everyone is to play. Some games will be quick to play while others (like Monopoly) may be very long. Try to pick the short games first so everyone can engage. Make sure that there are games that younger people can play successfully. Save the longer and more challenging games for when the time is right. Common types of games to consider include:

Board Games include Candy Land, Chutes and Ladders, checkers, chess, backgammon, scrabble, Trivial Pursuit, Clue, Life, Risk, Hungry Hippos, Jenga, Yahtzee, Catan, Cards Against Humanity or can be physically active games like Twister. If you have games like these around then it is fun to pull them out and play. But don't spend money to buy new games – many are fun that cost almost nothing, like the following:

Spoons – Spoons is a fun, fast moving game with 3-13 people. Materials needed are a deck of cards (Jokers removed) and one spoon for everyone, minus one. The object of the game is to get 4 cards of a kind and then grab a spoon; whoever doesn't grab a spoon earns a letter in the word "spoons": first "S", then "P", etc. Someone earns a letter each round. Players are out of the game once they have spelled "spoons." Directions: Everyone sits around the table or in a circle on the floor. Put all the spoons in the middle. The dealer passes out four cards to each player. The dealer keeps the rest of the cards in a pile on the table. At the beginning of each round, the dealer takes a card off the top of the deck then removes one card from their hand and passes it face down to the player on their left. This continues around the circle of players with each player taking a card from the person on their right who chooses whether to keep it and passes one card on to the next player. Each player discards to the person on their left. The faster this is done, the more fun it is. The last player places his discarded card into a discard pile and the next round begins when the dealer picks up a new card. If at any time the draw cards run out, reshuffle the trash pile and keep going. Players move closer to elimination each time they don't get a spoon and add another letter in the word S-P-O-O-N. The winner is the last player remaining. Here is a link that describes the game in more detail: https://www.itsalwaysautumn.com/how-to-play-spoons-card-game.html and here are a couple of YouTube that shows the game being played: https://www.youtube.com/watch?v=p8FZl5leLb4 and https://www.youtube.com/watch?v=P5apwK711_8 or https://www.youtube.com/watch?v=zyrxFg8emtg

Cards: Crazy 8s, UNO, Hearts, Poker, Magic, War, Euchre, Rummy, Gin, Spades, Canasta and tons more. Here are a few card rule websites in case you need reminders on how to play some of the games, as there are too many to list here.
https://www.pagat.com/alpha/
https://www.considerable.com/entertainment/card-games/card-games/
https://playingcarddecks.com/blogs/all-in/40-great-card-games-for-all-occasions
https://bicyclecards.com/rules/

Reading Our Life Is Like a Boardgame By Forever Small

Our life is like a board game
Every piece plays a part
We go back spaces

Or move ahead
It depends on what we do
And what we have said
Each of us is a player
Stepping on the tiles that create our long journey through life
Sometimes when we go back we learn how to move ahead
We are each pawns in the board game of our world
All different colors
We play the same game, but each of us experience a different story
Our life is like a board game.

http://www.teenink.com/poetry/free_verse/article/511825/Our-Life-is-like-a-Board-Game/

Day 17 Planning the Feastival

Description: A feastival is a combination of a feast and a festival! It combines the best components of traditional holiday celebrations – food and fun! A feastival is designed to bring together family, friends and neighbors in the sharing of food, and music. Feastivities are designed to bring joy. As families plan for the arrival of Santa Claus, creating a feastival around his coming can make it even more delightful. This activity brings the entire family together to make plans about what everyone thinks would make for a special event in preparation for the arrival of Santa.

Materials & Execution: Gather together and discuss what everyone thinks would be important to include in this special event. Successful gatherings can occur spontaneously, but often work better with a bit of planning. Everyone in the family can contribute ideas, so make this an open and fun conversation. Elements to include:

Food - What foods does the family think should be included? Who will make what? Open up opportunities to have everyone cooking or making something. It will generate more togetherness in the kitchen, more fun, conversation, and memory-making.

Music - Putting music on while people cook or get together helps promote a festive atmosphere! Designate someone to be in charge of keeping the music going. This is a big task, one that teens are very good at organizing!

Guests - Making a guest list and inviting people to come is important for your planning, and theirs. You want to make sure you have enough food and space to make everyone comfortable. You may also want to consider personalities and make decisions on how to increase chances for positivity between everyone to show the Santa Spirit.

Activities – While everyone is waiting for Santa to arrive, give them things to do. Options can include playing games, making crafts, doing puzzles, theatrical renditions, or story-telling. Have available different things so that people of all ages can participate.

Decorations - Even if you've decorated for the holiday, some last minute decorating will generate greater anticipation and excitement for the event. This could include lights, table settings, wreaths, or things that bring you delight.

Old traditions - Families may share sweet traditions that they want to keep going. Have a conversation about what they are and how to keep or transform them. There may be some old traditions that you want to let go of if they no longer serve you well.

New rituals - Families grow and change, so traditions should too! What are new rituals and traditions that you want to create? No time like the present to create them!

Planning for Santa - What are everyone's expectations about what should occur when Santa comes? Finding this out ahead of time is important for parents so they can be attentive to the details. Making magic takes a little pre-planning...

Reading: Happy Holiday by Irving Berlin Music Corp.

Happy Holiday, Happy Holiday
While the merry bells keep ringing
May your every wish come true
Happy Holiday, Happy Holiday
May the calendar keep bringing
Happy Holidays to you
It's the holiday season
And Santa Claus is coming back
The Christmas snow is white on the ground
When old Santa gets into town
He'll be coming down the chimney, down
Coming down the chimney, down
It's the holiday season
And Santa Claus has got a toy
For every good girl and good little boy
He's a great big bundle of joy
He'll be coming down the chimney, down
He'll have a big fat pack upon his back
And lots of goodies for you and me
So leave a peppermint stick for old St. Nick
Hanging on the Christmas tree
It's the holiday season

With the whoop-de-do and hickory dock
And don't forget to hang up your sock
'Cause just exactly at 12 o'clock
He'll be coming down the chimney
Coming down the chimney
Happy Holiday, Happy Holiday
While the merry bells keep bringing
Happy Holidays to you

Day 18 If I Was Santa

Description: The emphasis for this activity is to consider how to contribute the Santa Spirit to the community. Have everyone take a few minutes to write or draw their answer to the question - **If I was Santa, what would I want to deliver?** This activity can inspire us to think about how to make the world a better place. Maybe Santa wants to bring world peace or food so nobody will be hungry. Perhaps a vaccine for COVID-19 or for the town to have a new park where people could play soccer. It could be that we want Santa to deliver a bus that ran on time or an escalator that worked. The goal is to think about not just what Santa could put in our stocking but what Santa could bring that would benefit everyone. This exercise has been used by the Abraham Lincoln Memorial Library as a contest for students to answer. You can find information about some of the If I Was Santa contest entries on its Facebook page at https://www.facebook.com/pg/Lincoln.Museum/photos/?tab=album&album_id=10151342720901469

Materials & Execution: Have paper, pens, crayons or markers available. Ask everyone to answer the question **If**

I was Santa, what would I want to deliver? Then take turns reading of telling them! While there will be funny answers, try to build into the conversation the theme of bringing the Santa Spirit into the world.

Reading: I'd Like to Teach the World to Sing by the New Seekers

> I'd like to build the world a home
> And furnish it with love
> Grow apple trees and honey bees
> And snow white turtle doves
> I'd like to teach the world to sing
> In perfect harmony
> I'd like to hold it in my arms
> And keep it company
> I'd like to see the world for once
> All standing hand in hand
> And hear them echo through the hills
> For peace throughout the land
> (That's the song I hear)
> I'd like to teach the world to sing
> In perfect harmony
> I'd like to teach the world to sing
> In perfect harmony
> I'd like to build the world a home
> And furnish it with love
> Grow apple trees and honey bees
> And snow white turtle doves

> I'd like to teach the world to sing
> In perfect harmony
> I'd like to hold it in my arms
> And keep it company

Day 19 Trimming the Tree

Description: One of the central activities of the Santa season is setting up the tree and decorating it. Some families go out and chop down their own tree, others buy one from a local vendor, others have an artificial tree they put up every year, while some may string lights or baubles on plants or even make a tree out of cardboard or draw one on paper to put on the wall. It doesn't matter what the tree is made of – what matters is the joy of decorating of it. Making a tree beautiful can be a glorious family-bonding activity. Trimming the tree, along with enjoying some hot chocolate and warm cookies while festive music plays, can make for fond Santa Spirit memories that last a lifetime.

Materials & Execution: You need some sort of tree, a stand or way to keep it up, lights, garlands, ornaments or decorations. Ornaments can be made out of about anything, like pine cones, dried flowers, seashells, or old small toys. Adding paint, ribbons, glitter can make them especially beautiful.

Dough Ornaments: These are easy to make and all you need is 4 cups flour, 1 cup salt and 1 ½ cups warm water.

Mix them together into a dough that you can handle and then shape into whatever you want. Roll or pat the dough flat and have people put their hand or foot prints on them and let them dry to have a forever reminder of how small children were. Or mold them into snow people, round balls, cut them into designs like bones for dog ornaments. Poke a hole with a toothpick or straw before baking them at a 300-degree oven until they are firm, maybe an hour. Paint them, add names add glitter, and let your creativity fly! Details can be found at websites like https://wholefully.com/make-salt-dough-ornaments/ or on Youtubes like https://www.yummytoddlerfood.com/activities/the-best-salt-dough-ornaments/

Reading: Excerpts from **Christmas Trees** by Robert Frost

>...A stranger to our yard, who looked the city...
>He sat and waited till he drew us out
>A-buttoning coats to ask him who he was.
>He proved to be the city come again
>To look for something it had left behind
>And could not do without and keep its Christmas.
>He asked if I would sell my Christmas trees;
>My woods—the young fir balsams like a place
>Where houses all are churches and have spires.
>I hadn't thought of them as Christmas Trees.
>I doubt if I was tempted for a moment
>To sell them off their feet to go in cars
>And leave the slope behind the house all bare,

Where the sun shines now no warmer than the moon...
I dallied so much with the thought of selling.
Then whether from mistaken courtesy
And fear of seeming short of speech, or whether
From hope of hearing good of what was mine, I said,
"There aren't enough to be worthwhile."
"I could soon tell how many they would cut, You let me
look them over."
"You could look. But don't expect I'm going to let you
have them."
Pasture they spring in, some in clumps too close
That lop each other of boughs, but not a few
Quite solitary and having equal boughs
All round and round. The latter he nodded "Yes" to,
Or paused to say beneath some lovelier one,
With a buyer's moderation, "That would do.."...
We climbed the pasture on the south, crossed over,
And came down on the north. He said, "A thousand."
"A thousand Christmas trees!—at what apiece?"
He felt some need of softening that to me:
"A thousand trees would come to thirty dollars."
Then I was certain I had never meant
To let him have them. Never show surprise!
But thirty dollars seemed so small beside
The extent of pasture I should strip, three cents
(For that was all they figured out apiece),
Three cents so small beside the dollar friends...
Would pay in cities for good trees like those,
Regular vestry-trees whole Sunday Schools
Could hang enough on to pick off enough.

> A thousand Christmas trees I didn't know I had!
> Worth three cents more to give away than sell,
> As may be shown by a simple calculation.
> Too bad I couldn't lay one in a letter.
> I can't help wishing I could send you one,
> In wishing you herewith a Merry Christmas.

Parent processing recommendation: Here is a commentary for discussion with children about the poem. A city man wants to buy 1000 of Robert Frost's trees for three cents each in 1916. Frost had a relationship with the trees as living beings and never thought about them as Christmas trees until then. He and the man look at the trees and talk. Frost comes to the conclusion that he will not sell them for so little to people who would not understand the lives and meaning of the trees. Frost writes that he wishes he could send his friends in a letter not a tree but their meaning that he had discovered as he stood at this fork in the road. Frost is famous for also writing the poem, The Road Less Taken, which describes how he has taken the path less traveled, "and that has made all the difference."

Day 20 Book Trees

Description: Making holiday trees out of magazines or old paperback books is easy, quick, fun, and very rewarding! Since old magazines or paperback books can be easily found, the only expense for this project is paint to decorate them – and that is optional! These only take a few minutes to make and provide lasting enjoyment as decorations.

Materials & Execution: You need magazines or old paperback books, glue, glitter (optional) and paint (spray paint is best; gold, green, silver). Remove outer covers from the magazine or book, leaving just the pages. Fold the upper right-hand corner of the first page and bring it down so that the top edge of the page rest against the binding of the magazine. Crease this fold. Then take this page and fold it over until the crease rests against the binding of the magazine. Crease again, then fold the triangle (that overlaps the bottom of the magazine) upward so it will be even with the bottom of the book, crease it. The first page is finished. Continue folding & creasing the remaining pages. When all the pages of the book or magazine are folded, glue the front and back pages together. Spray tree with paint, and sprinkle glitter while still wet. Glue decorations or a star on it. Here are some

Youtubes to give you visuals: https://www.youtube.com/watch?v=TGlAe3oxA98 or https://www.youtube.com/watch?v=duHlUQNKy5o

Trees can be made out of books - https://www.countryliving.com/diy-crafts/g3923/christmas-trees-made-out-of-books/ or old pieces of Cardboard : https://www.youtube.com/watch?v=Wy6eMA3JmSE
https://www.youtube.com/watch?v=2J0I9jgey2c

Reading: Stopping by Woods on a Snowy Evening by Robert Frost

> Whose woods these are I think I know.
> His house is in the village though;
> He will not see me stopping here
> To watch his woods fill up with snow.
> My little horse must think it queer
> To stop without a farmhouse near
> Between the woods and frozen lake
> The darkest evening of the year.
> He gives his harness bells a shake
> To ask if there is some mistake.
> The only other sound's the sweep
> Of easy wind and downy flake.
> The woods are lovely, dark and deep,
> But I have promises to keep,
> And miles to go before I sleep,
> And miles to go before I sleep.

Day 21 Santa Movie Marathon

Description: Everyone has a favorite holiday movie, so picking just one can be hard. Of course, you can pick one each night for family viewing, or you can do a Santa Movie Marathon and see how many different movies about Santa can we watch in a day.

Materials & Execution: If you have a television, there are often Santa or holiday movies playing on channels in December. Or if you have DVDs or the ability to show films from Netflix, YouTube, On-Demand, or other stream services, then you have lots of choices. Here are some movie ideas to inspire you:

The Santa ClausThe Grinch
Santa Claus: The Movie The Polar Express
Miracle on 34th StreetRudolph the Red Nosed Reindeer
Christmas VacationA Christmas Story
White ChristmasLove Actually
A Christmas CarolPrancer
Home AloneElf
And don't forget the popcorn!

Reading: Movie Quotes of Note

"CHRISTMAS DOESN'T COME FROM A STORE. MAYBE CHRISTMAS PERHAPS MEANS A LITTLE BIT MORE."
*"CHRISTMAS WILL ALWAYS BE AS LONG AS WE STAND
HEART TO HEART AND HAND IN HAND."*
Dr. Seuss, author of The Grinch

"Seeing is believing but sometimes the most real things in the world
are the things we can't see."

The Polar Express

'To me, you are perfect".
Love Actually

"God Bless Us, Everyone."
A Christmas Carol

Parent processing recommendation: Have family members mention their own favorite holiday movie quotes!

Day 22 Lifting Our Voices

Description: Caroling, or singing together, is an ancient way of celebrating winter holidays. Singing is fun. It is a tangible example of the art of team-work. Some of us have high voices, some have low, deep voices and together we make beautiful music. It doesn't really matter how it sounds if we are joyfully lifting our voices up. Elf actor Will Farrell says the best way to spread Christmas cheer is singing loud for all to hear.[1] We can do a sing-along at home, but we can also go into the streets and sing to our neighbors or sing as we walk down the sidewalks past stores. Contact shelters, retirement homes, hospitals, or other places to see if they would allow you to come sing and bring cheer to residents who can't otherwise get out. And you can always sing just to yourself, to the dog and cat, or even to the plants. Something magical happens to us when we sing!

Materials & Execution: Most people don't know the words to all the Santa songs. We only hear them once a year and may know a few stanzas. In order to make beautiful music together, print copies of the words. This way you will be assured that we will all be singing the same words at the same time! It could be that someone has downloaded music that everyone can sing along to, or perhaps someone is playing the piano, flute, autoharp, or guitar and can guide others along. But accompanying music is not necessary! It helps if someone in the group knows the tune and has a powerful enough voice to guide others of us who "can't carry a tune in a bucket". It doesn't matter if people sing off-key. What matters is that we sing! In the Santa Spirit, it may be best to pick songs that everyone can sing and relate to. Selecting religious type songs may alienate people who don't share that particular faith. There are many secular Santa holiday songs that everyone can enjoy. Here are some:

Jingle BellsSilver Bells
Frosty The SnowmanWinter Wonderland
Sleigh RideMust Be Santa
Deck the HallsRudolph the Red Nosed Reindeer
Jingle Bell RockHere We Go a Wassailing
My Favorite ThingsSuzy Snowflake
Let It SnowSleigh Ride
No Place Like Home for the Holidays The Most Wonderful Time of the Year
Must be SantaToyland

Reading: The Twelve Days of Christmas by Linnea Asplind Riley

On the first day of Christmas My true love gave to me A partridge in a pear tree.

On the second day of Christmas My true love gave to me Two turtle doves And a partridge in a pear tree.

On the third day of Christmas My true love gave to me Three French hens, Two turtle doves
And a partridge in a pear tree.

On the fourth day of Christmas My true love gave to me Four calling birds, Three French hens,
Two turtle doves And a partridge in a pear tree.

On the fifth day of Christmas My true love gave to me Five golden rings, Four calling birds,
Three French hens, Two turtle doves And a partridge in a pear tree.

On the sixth day of Christmas My true love gave to me Six geese a-laying, Five golden rings,
Four calling birds, Three French hens, Two turtle doves And a partridge in a pear tree.

On the seventh day of Christmas My true love gave to me Seven swans a-swimming, Six geese a-laying, Five golden rings, Four calling birds, Three French hens, Two turtle doves And a partridge in a pear tree.

On the eighth day of Christmas My true love gave to me Eight maids a-milking, Seven swans a-swimming, Six geese a-laying, Five golden rings, Four calling birds, Three French hens, Two turtle doves And a partridge in a pear tree.

On the ninth day of Christmas My true love gave to me Nine ladies dancing, Eight maids a-milking, Seven swans a-swimming, Six geese a-laying, Five golden rings, Four calling birds,

Three French hens, Two turtle doves And a partridge in a pear tree.

On the tenth day of Christmas My true love gave to me Ten lords a-leaping, Nine ladies dancing,
Eight maids a-milking, Seven swans a-swimming, Six geese a-laying, Five golden rings, Four calling birds, Three French hens, Two turtle doves And a partridge in a pear tree.

On the eleventh day of Christmas My true love gave to me Eleven pipers piping, Ten lords a-leaping, Nine ladies dancing, Eight maids a-milking, Seven swans a-swimming, Six geese a-laying, Five golden rings, Four calling birds, Three French hens, Two turtle doves And a partridge in a pear tree.

On the twelfth day of Christmas My true love gave to me Twelve drummers drumming, Eleven pipers piping, Ten lords a-leaping, Nine ladies dancing, Eight maids a-milking, Seven swans a-swimming, Six geese a-laying, Five golden rings, Four calling birds, Three French hens, Two turtle doves And a partridge in a pear tree.

Day 23 The Santa Stocking

Description: This activity is designed to help to find the Santa Spirit in ourselves and in one another. Everyone is to write on slips of paper different things about what they appreciate for each member. If we get nothing else in our stocking from Santa, we will find many reminders from everyone in the family about how wonderful they think we are.

Materials & Execution: Have a stocking available, or materials to make one, whether out of fabric or paper. Have markers, pens, pencils or crayons, and slips of paper, approximately 2 inches long. The leader announces like:

"We all get so busy during the year that we forget to tell each other about all the things they do that make our lives better. Tonight we are going to take a few moments to write down things we enjoy about each other on these slips of paper. You can put one thing on each paper, so for any one person you may have two, five, or a dozen different slips of paper that says something you appreciate about them. You can draw pictures if you want. Then when you finish writing, fold the paper up and then put it into their stocking down in the toe. Since there are five of us, we will do this for each person. That means that each one of us will get on Christmas morning (or whenever Santa comes) reminders about why we love each other. For instance, for Grandma, I could write "I love that you send me recipes on how to make your favorite casserole." Or "I like to walk your dog because he's so cute". Do you have questions about what we are going to do?"

When you're finished writing, put the slips of paper into the stocking of the person you are writing about. Put the pieces of paper in the right person's stocking!

Reading: The Legend of the Santa Stocking by Yvonne Vissing

The snow was so deep that it slipped into the top of the boots Child wore while trudging home from school. Twinkle lights in the apartment window were a welcome sight. Pulling off wet well-worn socks, one big toe popped out. The stocking went flying across the room and landed near the fireplace where younger brother and little sister were setting up a board game.

"What's the matter?" Auntie ask as she hung silver tinsel onto the boughs of their tiny Christmas tree.

"That sock's no good. Too many holes - it can't be mended again."

"Maybe you can ask Santa for new socks," she suggested.

"Who wants socks for Christmas?" Child grumbled.

"Well, your dad says we're all going to put out our stockings for Santa tomorrow. You never know what you could find in it."

"I can't find the one I had last year. Besides, I probably won't get anything anyway."

"Grouchy, grouchy, grouchy" Brother teased.

"I believe Santa will remember ME," Sister proclaimed.

"Your mom is in the kitchen baking cookies so he'd better come," Auntie laughed.

Child started to stomp into the kitchen but Auntie ran to stand in front of the doorway.

"Shhhh.... Your mom and dad are in there finishing a discussion."

"Money talk again? Or rather, no money talk?" Child sighed with pursed lips.

"Oh, I think they're taking stock of their ins and outs," Auntie said. She hesitated, then continued, "I'm sure things are harder since I had to move in here with you all."

About that time, Mother came out with a plate of cookies, still steaming from the oven. "Hey, everybody! Get them while they're hot!"

Looking at Child's pouty face, she asked, "What's wrong?"

Child frowned. "Santa isn't coming."

"Why would you say such a thing?"

"Because." Child paused then continued, upset. "Because I don't do anything right. Because I'm not smart or cute or cool. Because nobody likes me. Because I'm not good enough. Because nobody cares. Because we live here. Because we don't have any money. Because."

"Wow. That's how it feels?" Mother gently rubbed Child's shoulder.

"That's how it is," Child asserted.

"You might want to take stock of yourself," Father suggested as he came in with a box of lights for the tree. "It might be time to examine your good qualities too. How you feel depends on what you want to take stock in."

"Things are not always as they seem," Mother agreed. "Tomorrow is Christmas Eve. Pick up your things, hang up your stocking, and tomorrow will be better. You'll see."

"No, things won't ever be better," Child sighed, as day turned into night.

* * *

As the children slept the snow fell. The adults snored. No one heard when the sock was whisked up the chimney. No one saw when it flew like a fairy through the snowflakes in the black, starlit sky. But someone knew where it went. Someone knew the stocking had value. Someone knew its importance was far from over. Someone knew its journey was just beginning...

* * *

It was Christmas Eve morning and for once the alarm clock didn't shout "Get up!" Everyone was sleeping in, everyone except for Child, who decided to get up early to make Christmas cards since "that's all I've got to give for presents." The floor was cold. Child searched for last night's socks and found the holeless sock left beside the bed. But where was the one thrown by the fire?

Suddenly, Child froze in place. A sock was there, but it was not like the one thrown there. Instead of the sock being torn and tattered, the holes had been replaced with shiny red and green threads that made it longer. Colorful sparkles and sequins glittered the stocking from top to bottom. It was bigger too, with a wide white fuzzy top. Gently picking it up, Child saw pieces of the old sock woven into the elegant stocking. How did this happen?

When the family awakened, Child excitedly greeted them with "Lookie! Look what happened to my stocking! Do you do this?"

No one knew how this transformed stocking came to be.

As the family cooked and cleaned to get ready for Santa's arrival, Child tried to figure out how the old sock turned into something so glorious.

Father helped Brother and Sister find their stockings and put them out for Santa Claus. Mother put out the ones she and Father had since they were little.

"I'll put out this one," Child announced while carrying over the transformed sock to the fireplace.

"I don't have a stocking", Auntie said. "So I decided to make my own". She paused and called out, "Gather round, everybody. I want to talk with you."

She walked over to the table and put out a stack of paper and markers. They surrounded the table to see what she was up to.

"I have a present for you all," Auntie announced. Everyone was surprised. Auntie had moved in with them because she had no money. So how did she come up with a present for them?

"Life has been pretty challenging for me in this year and I want to thank you for letting me move in with you. I know it's been an adjustment for everyone. Sometimes I don't tell you how much I appreciate you. So I thought tonight was the right time. I'm going to take pieces of paper and write things that I think are really awesome about each one of you and put it into your stockings. Then tomorrow morning, no matter what else you get, you will find reminders from me about how remarkable I think you are."

"I wondered if you wanted to write each other notes to remind each other of all the nice things you do for each other too."

"That's a great idea! I know I get so busy at work that sometimes I forget to tell you all how much I love you. I'm in!" Father replied.

"Me too!" Mother agreed.

"But what should we write?" Child asked.

Auntie smiled. "For instance, in your mom's stocking, I'm going to put in these different slips of paper. This one says: 'You always make time to listen to me'. Others say 'it's really fun to play cards with you', 'you have a beautiful smile', 'thank you for being patient', and 'I love your eggplant parm.'"

"So we can put in more than one thing?" Brother wanted to know.

"You bet! I'm putting in a bunch for each one of you. There are so many wonderful things about each one of you, I couldn't write them on just one slip of paper. I'm going to put in as many as I can until my hand gets tired," she winked.

"So you want us to write down reasons we love each other?" little Sister asked.

"Exactly," Auntie smiled.

"I want to do that!" Sister was bouncing with glee. "If I don't know how to write the words, can I draw pictures of what you do?" she asked.

"What a cool idea!" Mother grinned. "I think I'll also put in wishes for what I want for you as you grow up," she added. "I want more than anything for you to be happy and healthy."

"I'm going to put in some IOUs," Father declared. "For instance, over the holidays I promise to take you all to the movies. And skating. I will put that in because I enjoy spending time with you."

"Only put nice, not naughty, stuff," Brother reminded. "We've all got good things inside us."

"Absolutely" everyone agreed.

Auntie passed out the paper and markers and everyone started writing furiously. One by one, pieces of paper were tucked in each other's stockings.

Sister observed, "Our stockings are already so full there won't be any room for Santa to put anything!"

"That's pretty fine that we think we're all so awesome. But I bet Santa will find room to put some things in your stockings anyway," Mother laughed.

After dinner Mother put on holiday music and the family gathered together around the tree to put out their stockings. Father got the book ready for the annual reading of "The Night Before Christmas" poem.

* * *

Christmas morning arrived and the children woke with glee.

"He came!"

"Let's go open our stockings!"

"Come on! Hurry up!"

Everyone dashed to their stockings and picked up their bulging socks. Sure enough, their stockings were brimming full of toys, books, art supplies, snacks, harmonicas and sweets, along with the pieces of paper they had written on the night before.

"Let's save the notes until last and read them to each other," Brother suggested, with his mouth already full of chocolate.

"Yes, let's!"

"Great idea!"

After examining their toys, trinkets and sweets, there was a mound of paper in front of everyone's stocking, begging to be read.

"I want to see what nice things everyone said about me," Sister bounced. "Will you read them to me?"

"Of course," Father agreed.

"Me first!!" Sister shouted. Everyone laughed.

"Why don't we take turns so we can see what's in each other's stockings?" Auntie suggested. And that's exactly what they did.

Brother clapped when he looked at Sister's picture of him playing a board game. "I love it when you play with me."

"See my picture of us at the beach? You taught me how to get my face wet and hold my breath. That was fun. Can we go again next summer?" Sister begged.

"Sure, Sis. Will do. Did you get my note about how I like it when you scratch my itchy back? And that I love it when you are always waiting to hug me when I get home from school?" And then Sister threw her arms around Brother, tumbling him over while everyone giggled.

"Thanks for letting me know you like it when we go on bike rides," Dad smiled at Brother. "I like riding my bike and enjoy your company. When it gets warm, let's check our tires so we can go more places together."

"Cool! I like spending time with you too. Did you see my paper telling you I'd like it if you'd let me show me how you take photographs? Yours are always awesome," Brother said.

Soon the family was learning new information about what each other enjoyed. Each slip of paper revealed something about each other they may not have realized.

"I never knew that you all felt these ways," Mother confessed as she looked at the pieces of paper piled on the rug. "Sometimes I guess I've been too busy to notice or ask you about what's going on. Isn't this a wonderful gift to find out all the things we really like about each other?"

"I'm gonna cry, you all said such nice things to me," Auntie said as she wiped away happy tears from her eyes. "I thought maybe I was imposing too much by having to live with you."

"Silly Auntie, you're the best auntie in the world!" Little sister said as she leaped across the room and threw her arms around Auntie's neck and planted a big kiss on her cheek.

"We agree!" everyone said in spontaneous unison, at which everyone burst into laughter.

Child was the quietest of all. Family members had put in notes that said Child was "beloved", "smart", "funny", "kind", "responsible", "dependable", "hard-working", "nice", and "a good role model for us all". "You are the heart of our family," one note said. "I want to grow up to be like you," said another. Laughter erupted over the pictures Sister had drawn.

How could last night have felt so bad and today feel so good? Child was extra perplexed to find tucked into the toe of the stocking a new pair of socks surrounded by a note that read, "feet are the foundation for your journey ahead."

"What do you think that means?" Mother wondered.

"Ah, Christmas is full of miracles and magic," Auntie observed.

Child sat quietly, thinking.

Mountains of paper notes described the many reasons and ways people loved each other. "I love you because… I love you when you do… I love you when you don't do…. I am grateful for… I appreciate…. I enjoy….It's fun when we…. I like it when…. Could we…." The lists were never ending. Each person's heart swelled with joy and delight.

There were also wishes for peace on earth, goodwill to all people everywhere. "All that starts with your being nice to each other," Father couldn't help but to remind them.

Sister hugged her stocking and then ran around the room from person to person, hugging them singing, "You love me, you love me, you think I'm wonderful…". Everyone chuckled with delight, because they felt the same way.

"Of all the things I got, these are my favorite presents," Brother declared. "You couldn't buy these in a store. These are all about us, from us to us, heart to heart. They're original, just like us!"

"This is the best Christmas ever," Mother observed. "Shall we make writing reminders about how special we are to each other part of our annual Christmas Eve tradition?"

"YES!" It was unanimous. And that was the beginning of our Santa stocking note giving tradition.

**

The rest of Christmas day was spent cooking and feasting

while listening to music and talking. The spirit of play and gratitude filled the hours as evening drew near.

"Hey Auntie, that was a great present you gave us. How did you think of it?" Child caressed the stocking and appeared to be looking for its message, like reading it was coded in Braille.

She smiled. "You know, that old sock of yours got me thinking. It's a good thing you didn't throw it away. It reminded us that we're all more than it may seem. We all got flaws and holes. We're not perfect, but every one of us has the potential to be something else, something bigger and better. We only put into the stocking reminders about what is wonderful about each other. The presents we gave each other aren't giving us something new but are merely reminders for us to see all the gifts we have inside."

Child silently considered that thought, then asked, "Where do you think my stocking really came from?"

"That I do not know. I guess Santa was saw what you needed most this Christmas. Maybe you needed something to help you look at yourself and others differently. You can be anything you want, you know."

"Are you Santa?" Child asked.

"No. But I'm a pretty good elf," Auntie admitted.

***

Christmas night, after Brother and Sister fell happily exhausted into their beds, Father sat quietly with Child.

"So did you have a good Christmas?" he asked.

"It was the best," Child nodded. "I really appreciated the notes everybody wrote to let me know that I was important to them. The rest of the presents were cool, but it was so great to reach into the stocking and pull out slip after slip of reasons why people love me. I never knew I was that important to you all."

Father slipped his arm around Child's shoulder. "Oh, you're more important than you may ever know. I guess this Christmas everyone helped us to take stock of what's good about us. Love is always the best thing to give and take stock in."

Child suddenly blinked, sat up taller and then hopped up. He ran over and picked up the transformed stocking. "Do you think that's why they call this a Stock-In?"

They laughed together. And one more time before going to sleep, they pulled out the little slips of paper from their stockings and read the things others had written about how wonderful they are.

Parent response recommendation: Consider making this Santa Stocking activity part of your annual holiday events. It will focus members of the family to think about the abundance of ways people love us and shift the focus of the holiday away from material gifts.

Day 24 The Santa Feastival

Description: This is the moment we've been planning for! Santa is arriving in whatever form we envision him to be. He could arrive in person, in personS or in spirit. Creating a feastival around the sharing of the Santa Spirit – and maybe food and gifts - could occur on December 24, Christmas Eve, which is the traditional night when Santa Claus arrives. But it doesn't have to be then. The Santa Feastival could occur whenever the family wants as the culmination of Santa's arrival. A feastival is a gathering of family and friends who want to share a feast of delicious holiday foods and hold a festival of merriment and good cheer.

Materials & Execution: At Day 17 in this book of activities, family members focused on what they wanted to bring, make and do at the Feastival. Now is the time to implement those plans! Each family member or friend brings something to contribute to either the feast or the festivities of the evening. The trick for this to go smoothly is good planning. Having everyone engaged and deciding what they are going to contribute ahead of time makes it easier for the host to orchestrate the feastival in a timely and Santa-spirited way. The Dec 17 the activity was to organize each member of the family to figure out what they are going to contribute to the feastivity. Reducing last minute stress is vital, as stress over not having a key ingredient for what people want to create can torpedo what would otherwise be a super family moment. Remember – the key is making happy memories, so we want to avoid making sad or stress whenever possible. As a reminder, key ingredients for a fantastic feastival include:

Delicious and special foods

Decorations

Great, positive conversations

Music to listen to or sing together

Activities to do, whether

Maybe presents to open or share

Arrival of special guests (which could include a Santa figure)

And most importantly, the Santa Spirit!

Reading: The Night Before Christmas by Clement Clarke Moore

'Twas the night before Christmas, when all through the house
Not a creature was stirring, not even a mouse;
    The stockings were hung by the chimney with care,
    In hopes that St. Nicholas soon would be there;
    The children were nestled all snug in their beds;
    While visions of sugar-plums danced in their heads;

And mamma in her 'kerchief, and I in my cap,
Had just settled our brains for a long winter's nap,
When out on the lawn there arose such a clatter,
I sprang from my bed to see what was the matter.
Away to the window I flew like a flash,
Tore open the shutters and threw up the sash.
The moon on the breast of the new-fallen snow,
Gave a cluster of midday to objects below,
When what to my wondering eyes did appear,
But a miniature sleigh and eight tiny rein-deer,
With a little old driver so lively and quick,
I knew in a moment he must be St. Nick.
More rapid than eagles his coursers they came,
And he whistled, and shouted, and called them by name:
"Now, *Dasher*! now, *Dancer*! now *Prancer* and *Vixen*!
On, *Comet*! on, *Cupid*! on, *Donner* and *Blitzen*!
To the top of the porch! to the top of the wall!
Now dash away! dash away! dash away all!"
As leaves that before the wild hurricane fly,
When they meet with an obstacle, mount to the sky;
So up to the housetop the coursers they flew
With the sleigh full of toys, and St. Nicholas too—
And then, in a twinkling, I heard on the roof
The prancing and pawing of each little hoof.
As I drew in my head, and was turning around,
Down the chimney St. Nicholas came with a bound.
He was dressed all in fur, from his head to his foot,
And his clothes were all tarnished with ashes and soot;

A bundle of toys he had flung on his back,
And he looked like a peddler just opening his pack.
His eyes—how they twinkled! his dimples, how merry!
His cheeks were like roses, his nose like a cherry!
His droll little mouth was drawn up like a bow,
And the beard on his chin was as white as the snow;
The stump of a pipe he held tight in his teeth,
And the smoke, it encircled his head like a wreath;
He had a broad face and a little round belly
That shook when he laughed, like a bowl full of jelly.
He was chubby and plump, a right jolly old elf,
And I laughed when I saw him, in spite of myself;
A wink of his eye and a twist of his head
Soon gave me to know I had nothing to dread;
He spoke not a word, but went straight to his work,
And filled all the stockings; then turned with a jerk,
And laying his finger aside of his nose,
And giving a nod, up the chimney he rose;
He sprang to his sleigh, to his team gave a whistle,
And away they all flew like the down of a thistle.
But I heard him exclaim, ere he drove out of sight
"Happy Christmas to all, and to all a good night!"

www.ingramcontent.com/pod-product-compliance
Lightning Source LLC
Chambersburg PA
CBHW070935080526
44589CB00013B/1521